Unlock Your Potential with the Realities of Trading

Azeez Mustapha

ADVFN BOOKS

Contents

Introduction

USD GBP

Experience has shown that people want to keep doing what they're doing, while expecting different results. People hate to be told that they're wrong. They prefer their current ways of trading, even if those ways have proven to bring poor results for them. A trading career is all about identifying what doesn't work for you and stopping it.

You may be aware that people hate being told the truth, but in trading, truth is the only thing that can unlock your potential and liberate you. People don't want to hear this. It's very difficult, because many a trader thinks the market should respect their personal trading approach, even if it's a dangerous one. But this kind of mindset can't improve any statistics, as far as trading success is concerned. We think we love ourselves, but our trading approaches bring results that make us weep.

You can only unlock your potential through the realities of trading.

Our mind is our biggest enemy. Our mind prevents us from following our trading plans and deceives us into disobeying our winning rules because of some recent transitory drawdowns… And we thus miss great opportunities to make decent profits. We overrule our tested and trusted plans. We do things that go against our plans, such as not letting our profits run, exiting prematurely because we think we can't go broke taking a profit. Our mind deceives us into looking endlessly for the Holy Grail, which exists only within us. The grass is always greener on the other side of the fence. We think there is a guru somewhere who doesn't lose.

Your mind is the biggest obstacle that you need to overcome because without achieving that, you can't be a long-term winning trader. This is a game of the mind.

When you know how to condition your mind to approach trading properly, you will liberate yourself through trading realities.

In the game of speculation, resilience and courage are needed. Serenity, confidence and faithfulness to one's trading approach are often mentioned. But what about valour? We often neglect this, and most us fail because we lack the necessary valour that can propel us to breakthrough. We can't just leave a small profit alone until it becomes a bigger profit. Our mind begins to manipulate us in various ways and we will start to think that it is normal to take a small profit, rather than riding it until it becomes a bigger one. As an example: those who bought Bitcoin in early 2015 and have held it till now are doing much better than those who took their small profits too quickly. The logic in taking small profits too quickly reveals a great but flawed exit strategy because it shields us from our own shortcomings, and we're extremely good at doing stupid things while thinking we're geniuses.

You just need to keep doing the right things; although doing that isn't always comfortable.

These chapters have been previously published as articles on various blogs and forums.

Chapter 1: The Best Trader in the World

GBP EUR

"Life itself is a risky enterprise. Sometimes we fly high, enjoying great success. But then suddenly we fall into deep disappointments and the haunting reality of a failure, leaving our hearts wondering if there is anything worth looking forward to." – **Joe Stowell**

There are super traders all around the world. If you don't know them, I know some of them. They earn their livelihood by trading and they're financially free. Now the question is: Who's the best trader in the world? Indeed, the best trader exists. Now, I won't mention names, but I'll tell you how the best trader trades.

The best trader doesn't argue with the markets – he always admits his mistakes. Most people tend to feel they're right, even if facts prove them wrong. Extremely terrible speculators don't accept their errors. It's really a psychological condition that makes a person refuse to think he's made a mistake, even if reality shows otherwise. Being overconfident in riding a position that's determinedly negative is definitely not a good thing. Top traders always acknowledge their mistakes.

Likewise, the best trader may use any kind of positive expectancy system including fundamental strategies and anticipate that the market will move in a certain direction. If the price movement or fundamental figures happen to be against his expectation, he'll smooth all his positions immediately. No arguments, no hope.

Financial markets have no mercy upon anybody. If things go against you, then get out of the market without wasting time. Every good speculator I've studied is really good at cutting positions that seem to go determinedly against them. Yet, whenever the market proves them right, they run their gains for a considerable amount of time.

The greatest trader accepts the uncertainty that can affect any open orders; they even do this before they open the orders. Uncertainty remains our ally, since speculation is a game in its own right. Negativity is also included in the game. The best trader doesn't feel sad when a trade goes negative, nor does he feel too happy when a trade goes positive.

Using a System Profitably is Conditional

Are you a successful trader? Did you like the results you produced as a trader in the previous year? If not, what errors did you make and how can you improve your results henceforth? You may need a trading system that takes care of some cogent factors contributing to profitable trading. Do you have these factors in mind? Please consider some of them:

1. *Do I have a rule to follow in my speculative activities?* A trading strategy should be approached with the level of seriousness and enthusiasm with which one would approach any high level endeavour or business. The entry, exit, position sizing and other rules of this strategy must be followed to the letter.

2. *Do I have a worst-case emergency plan?* A good system should have a rule (or rules) that can deal with any adverse movements that can affect an open trade, as well as a rule that makes you exit quickly if things are no longer going in your favour.

3. *Do I have a positive expectancy system that can enable me to survive the current type of market?* A good system ought to make money in good market conditions and make as little drawdowns as possible in bad

markets conditions. It should have positive expectancy incorporated into it, which means that at least, two dollars should be expected for each dollar that is being risked. In other word, you should be profitable on a long-term basis even with only 30% accuracy.

4. *Do I have a technique that will continue working even if the market conditions change without warning?* Yes, a good trading system ought to survive all market conditions. A good trading system can work well in bull or bear markets. But maybe you should stay out of extremely consolidating markets! You just need to stick to its rules.

5. *Do I even recognize the current type of market?* It helps to be aware of the type of the market one is trading and the current prevailing condition of the market. This can help you make informed trading decisions.

6. *Do I constantly condition my mindset in a way that makes me execute my trades flawlessly?* You need to work on yourself. There are traders who use position sizing that is far bigger than the one recommended. Some enter additional trades based on analysis that is completely different from the rules of the system. Some do not even use stops at all – contrary to the system rule! A trader using a good system should learn how to control herself/himself and do the right things in the markets rather than doing things that would satisfy human emotions.

If you answered no to any of those questions, you have clues about why your results in the past have been undesirable. These, by the way, are only a few of the questions you could ask yourself. If you could take the factors above into consideration and work on them successfully, then you may find that trading can indeed be profitable.

Conclusion

When the markets go in our favour, we feel like a champion. We assume that we are a super trader and that we're smarter than other traders. In most cases, only traders who have experienced the good and the ugly sides of the markets and survived them all are those who are really qualified to be our mentors. You need to forget about your past and look forward to a brighter future. It's important that you overlook your past failures and press forward.

This chapter concludes with the quotes below:

"Stephen Covey says – 'Live out of your imagination, not your history'. Look forward, not in your rear view mirror – or you're sure to crash. It's not what happens to you, it's how you handle it that counts. Your mistakes are completely separate from who you are as a person. Take pride that you're moving one step closer towards your goals. Don't cripple your future growth by shooting yourself in the foot because you made a screw up." – Louise Bedford [paraphrased]

"One of the main issues that new traders have is that they have expectations of huge rewards in a short period of time. 'I'll take my $5,000 trading account and turn it into a million dollars in a year, and tell my boss where he can go!' That rate of return is a bit unrealistic. By increasing your account size just a couple of percentage points a month, the power of compound interest will make you wealthy, but over a long period of time. Trading as a career is a marathon, not sprint. Those who try to make too much too fast often over-leverage their account and take on unnecessary risks by doing so. One or two large losses can wipe out a few weeks or months of good gains! If you do that you have 'worked for free' as your account takes these major drawdowns. Does anyone want to work for free? I know I don't." – Rick Wright (Online Trading Academy)

Chapter 2: Trend Following

EUR CHF

"The trending market is an ideal market to trade and make money. What trend following is not is prediction or forecasting about how the markets will go. Trend following is based on reacting to price, price and again, price. It is not based on trying to predict price directions." – Michael Covel

Perhaps the most crucial aspect of the dynamics of the market is their current bias whose relevance is due to the reality that it causes the nexus between trend development and the mindset of both Smart Money and Dumb Money. Obviously, making secret purchases in a northbound market is far more upwards than secret purchases in a southbound market and shorting in a southbound market is far more downwards than shorting in a northbound market. Because of this, the dynamics of the market proffer crucial explanation of the popular 'trading mentality,' i.e. a field of study that attempts to write about market reactions by analysing the psychology of Smart Money and Dumb money. Owing to their characteristics, market biases proffer some speculative methods.

Biases happen any moment and, as such, they are what we need to realise desired gains. Vividly, the bias ought to be in place, therefore positions sometimes shouldn't be opened in an extremely bearish trend or smoothed in an extremely bullish trend. Trading against the extremely bullish trend or extremely bearish trend isn't the most crucial thing for a trader – the pundits of this style would merely have misguided you. The most crucial thing is the general trend. Our belief is that if a bias has started, it should keep on going. It's much more likely for that to hold than it is to be void, especially when positions have been opened. At times, a bias may last longer than expected. It can thus be challenging for speculators to keep on riding their profits when the bias still holds and not to exit based on fear.

When an analyst thinks a market is oversold, it isn't oversold. Being oversold or being overbought is simply something imaginary. This should be construed to mean something similar to a financial newscaster who announces that an economic item is rated a 'buy' due to a turning level. No matter how logical the explanation is, or the kind of 'degree' they hold, whether they're wearing a $5 tie or $50 tie, in most cases they'll only achieve 50% accuracy in their analyses. If they have gained more than that, it means that they short weak markets and buy bull markets.

An adept rule-based speculator enjoys more free time than a mechanical trader. Adeptness has to do with the tendency to go with the flow of the markets. Mean reversion speculation is anti-trend (selling in an uptrend and buying in a downtrend, looking for turning points). Many traders feel that an overextended bearish market could be ready to rally and do so protractedly. But the reality is that it might still fall by 600, 800, 1,000, 1,300 pips before it even goes up. One of the major reasons traders buy renowned and world-famous pairs is that analysts talk about them and investors are often aware of them. If the overextended market continues in the direction that people don't expect, then investors get whacked. As a result of this, everybody would be looking forward to strangling the prime economic forecaster, as investors holding other instruments are apprehensive. Invariably, you would see some suave ape in the media, often a forecaster whose studies were published in the previous year and adjusted some days prior to the occurrence, safeguarding his studies by reducing the likelihood while announcing that he still prefers the scenario since it remains overextended. Or it might be that the pair displays a temporary halt in its journey and some speculators feel it's now great to enter contrary to the established trend and realise gains in counter-trend or mean reversion trading.

They may not realise, but they've fallen in love with a wrong direction and would go on opening positions against the trend, usually with heavy losses, till they receive a margin call or forfeit their portfolio.

I've experimented seriously with over 120 trading ideas, but trend-following has stood the test of the time. Thomas Stridsman (CTA), who's been developing strategies for model-based investing since the early 1990s, declares that he's decided to do only trend-following. The notion behind this idea is plausible; anywhere the strongest trend is, that's where returns can easily be realised... For trading purposes, I've decided to do only trend-following. This kind of trading approach has proven timeless. We make gains while the trend is still extant.

Could I say I'm better than other traders? I feel I've an advantage in believing that any trader can be successful, myself included. That's what my methodology is all about. As a result of this, I shrug off all misleading moves and noises regularly. I'm not misled by incongruous financial data that have no long-term effect, since I stay focus on my time-tested analysis, which has to do with offering myself with high-risk, low-reward opportunities that would ensure my ultimate victory in the markets.

Those going with the flow of the markets are aware that even if a trend has been happening for a long time and they think there are still more gains to make, they may still trade in that direction, and as often as not, they'd win. Never forget that the Forex market is the best trending market that exists, and therefore the best trading method to use on it is trend-following. It's no secret that trading with the trend will normally provide the best results.

I conclude this chapter with these quotes:

"...A truly great trader will learn to take his money off the table and be satisfied with what he made. It is the greedy trader who overextends himself. It is the novice trader who fights the trend. It is an even greater novice who believes that there is such a thing as 'support.' – Joe Ross [Paraphrase]

"The trending market is arguably the type of market that best lends itself to being traded and offers the greatest earnings prospects... The trending market is an ideal market to trade and make money... You should only trade in the direction of the main trend" – Thomas Wacker

Chapter 3: The Cost of Discipline – Part 1

CHF CAD

We don't derive satisfaction just from gaining pips or through some elusive Holy Grail.

Disciplined traders get satisfaction from doing what they know is really right, even when they occasionally take losses. Some hate loss to the extent that, if loss were a person, he would be lynched. Only a lack of knowledge would make someone give up trading because of a losing streak – something that market wizards know is normal and they constantly anticipate and control successfully. Expert traders measure real satisfaction from their level of discipline, as futures gains and losses are measured in ticks, currency market gains and losses are measured in pips, and as those of stocks are measured in points.

There are different aims for different market speculators. Certain speculators focus on risk control or keeping roll-downs as low as possible (and some may want to double their account every week). But some traders are making attempts to combine huge profits with fewer roll-downs, for example fifty per cent per annum with no more than twenty per cent roll-down. No matter what you want, lot sizes are what should be used to attain your realistic trading goals. Given the importance of safe uses for lot sizes, all traders ought to take it seriously. Yet, in reality, many rookies and even experts don't bother much about this powerful tool. They prefer to focus on a magical methodology, trading instruments and market types. Though nothing is wrong with the aforementioned, they are ineffectual without the judicious use of lot sizes. Granted, a nice strategy helps you formulate sensible lot sizes in your trade; however, lot sizes are great in their own right. Why? By using lot sizes that are too big on small accounts, many traders have seen large roll-downs on those accounts even when they have superb strategies.

Why aren't we disciplined? Do you hate hearing that you are not disciplined? Well, without being disciplined, you'll eventually find it impossible to outsmart the markets. Trading success is simple only when we're disciplined do to what's right. We find trading success elusive because we can't be disciplined. Some know the grim consequences of certain hard drugs, but they still use them. We know certain types of junk foods are detrimental to our health, but we can't resist eating them. We know some lifestyles are dangerous, but we still live them. We know what things are morally wrong, but we find them appealing. We know the best ways to handle money, but do we do that? There are many more examples...

As long as the markets exist, there will be disciplined and undisciplined speculators. Undisciplined speculators trade rashly, but blame others. Being undisciplined means knowing the correct trading styles, but doing something suicidal.

Our ultimate goal is to make decent profits from the markets irrespective of what the markets do. In order to achieve this goal, there are trading principles that must be incorporated into our speculative activities. The reality, however, is that, it seems that the human mind isn't wired to be disciplined enough to do the right things.

How can we be disciplined? And what are the advantages that might be derived from this? The next chapter will talk more about it.

Conclusion

Although you can't change what has happened to you in the past, you can take steps to ensure your success in the future. All over the world, there are people that, regardless of their nationality, skin, colour, ethnicity, or language enjoy success in the markets. Yes, a bright future awaits serious traders!

The quote below ends this chapter:

"A trading system idea might look like it won't work, but the more knowledge you have about yourself, and the more you understand yourself, the better you'll be at determining whether you're looking at the truth or a belief. The systems that work in the markets are so much simpler than any I would have thought possible, and the potential returns are so much bigger." – Frank Eaves

Chapter 4: The Cost of Discipline – Part 2

CADJPY

"The truly successful traders are incredible discipline fanatics. Presumably, it's not even enough to be more disciplined than the average person. You just need to be in the top 10% group. Self-discipline causes the trader to place certain obligations on himself." – Christian Lukas

Being disciplined enough to do what is right in the markets doesn't always make us look smart. The trader who doesn't use stops may look smart when the price comes back to his entry level, yet he'll have no-one to blame but himself when the price on one pair/cross refuses to come back to its entry level. When do you think the AUDUSD will go back to the psychological level at 0.6000? The trader who uses stops may look stupid as he sustains small roll-downs on his accounts, especially when the price goes back in his direction after getting stopped out. Yet the stops will one day save him, his career and his nerves. Someone who uses excessively big position sizes may look cute when he gains huge profits with small price movements, but huge losses are possible with small price movements. Anyone who uses small position sizes to get small profits would be derided as using minuscule lots, whereas minuscule lots would lead to only negligible drawdowns in bad market conditions.

A trend follower needs self-control to ride his winners. Planting crops is similar to a long-term career in trading. A planter plants the seeds and employs patience for the ultimate results – harvesting. As the seeds grow, he patiently tends the sprouts. It takes as long as necessary for seeds to grow into trees. A speculator looks for a signal that meets his entry criteria and then opens a trade accordingly. He manages his trades until an exit criterion is fulfilled. A sane planter knows it's unrealistic to look for instant harvest, because certain conditions must be fulfilled before harvest can take place; neither can he force premature harvest. If a speculator misses a signal, he'll be disciplined enough to wait for a new signal. Trending markets are formidable: one should flow with them, not against them. The financial markets are thus formidable, so we need not resist its flow.

What should we do, then? We just need to be disciplined enough to avoid trading styles that aren't in our best interests and embrace those that ensure our long-term success. Trading psychologists help in achieving this. Are we disciplined enough to obey simple winning rules? Writer Julie A. Link said: "When I was young, I thought the cost of living in my parents' home was too high. Looking back, I laugh at how ridiculous it was to complain. My parents never charged me a cent for living at home. The only 'cost' was obedience. I simply had to obey rules like clean up myself, be polite, tell the truth… The rules weren't difficult, but I still had trouble obeying them. My parents didn't kick me out for my disobedience, however. They just kept reminding me that the rules were to protect me, not to harm me, and sometimes they made the rule stricter to protect me from myself." Successful trading rules are there to save your accounts and your nerves and to make you realise your goals in the end. These rules will be mentioned in future chapters.

Forex is a wonderful instrument because it rewards the disciplined. Disciplined traders have maintained crucial priorities in their career and they'll stick to other important aspects of trading. There are winning trading principles that have stood the test of the time, and disciplined traders stick to these principles even though the principles are not perfect. Disciplined traders believe they will be great in trading (with realistic expectations). They eventually become market wizards

Commending the Disciplined Trader

Your trading plan is clearly stated,
Offensive and defensive weapons are with you at the war front,
Profits come to you easily,
You are an expert who remains unperturbed
Survival is the real winnings
You react to profit and loss in the same way
No matter what your open orders do
Your experience helps in selecting great signals:
Here is your opportunity!
Please show them you are a victor
For you have always been victorious!

Conclusion

Can you now see why discipline is crucial to your success? To be aware of this is a great step towards your personal evolution as a successful trader. As it's often said, "To be conscious that you are ignorant is a great step to knowledge."

I conclude the chapter with a quote below:

"Trading is simple, but it isn't easy. There are many obstacles and challenges. Do you have that attitude of courage, tenacity, perseverance and determination to start each trade afresh, regardless of the outcome of the previous trade?" – Paul Wallace

Chapter 5: The Collapse of Two Big Financial Institutions

JPY NZD

"Now, if a trade moves against me, I'm out." – **Charles Kirk**

Many big and small financial institutions have collapsed – not just the two that are mentioned in this chapter. However, these two institutions are known to most well-informed fundamental analysts, especially those who also research past events in the financial world. They didn't collapse recently: their demise happened years ago, but there are great lessons traders, investors and fund managers can learn from their sad stories. When one falls into a pit he becomes a warning to others.

One of these institutions was Barings Bank (a merchant bank) which collapsed in 1995 and the other was Amaranth Advisors hedge fund, which collapsed in 2006. What can you know about these institutions? What led to their collapse? What can you learn from this? How can you prevent the collapse of your trading account/portfolios, no matter how small it is?

Barings Bank, founded and owned by the Baring family, existed between 1762 and 1995. It was the oldest investment bank in the UK. This great institution went to ruin, following an irrational gamble by Nick Leeson, an employee of the bank. He was caught on the wrong side of the markets and he refused to smooth his positions. Instead, he added more to his losers. He lost about $1.3 billion while engaging in futures trading at the bank's office located in Singapore. He was jailed and later released in 1999.

Amaranth Advisors LLC was a hedge fund whose assets were worth nine billion dollars before collapsing in 2006, having lost around five billion dollars. The fund made use of various strategies in speculation. It was founded by Nicholas Maounis and had its headquarters in Greenwich, Connecticut, USA. The person behind the colossal loss is a Canadian trader named Brian Hunter, whose irrational speculation on natural gas futures went awry. It was one of the biggest losses in trading history.

When One Falls Into a Pit he Becomes a Warning to Others

Many people want to hear that they're right even when the reality proves otherwise. But we should stop deceiving ourselves. It isn't good to trade in the wrong market direction, especially when the primary trend is against us. When there is a vivid downtrend on the chart, it can only mean one thing: the price is skydiving. What is the best direction to take when the price is falling?

On 31 December 2008, the USDCHF closed at 1.0669, whereas it closed at 0.9146 on 31 December 2012. Imagine what could have happened to someone who refused to close his long position or sought only long trades since 2008? Do you buy when your model signifies a 'sell?' Do you sell when your model signifies a 'buy?' Can you imagine how many pips the USDCHF has lost since 2008? There's no bad thing with a downtrend, on the condition that traders accept that a market is weak and speculate accordingly. We make money in bear markets only when we sell short.

A strong market forms a series of higher highs and higher lows, and conversely a weak market forms lower lows and lower highs. For refusal to follow the line of the least resistance, a trader whose account was very big now has a very small account (meaning the person is poorer). Trading accounts have imploded because of refusal to know when to hold onto a trade and when to cut a trade. For refusal to accept the reality of the markets, big financial institutions collapsed. It isn't uncommon for some instruments to continue their weakness even when good economic figures come out, and as a result of this, my experience has coerced me to trade according to what I see. It's imperative to know when some pairs/crosses should be bought and when they should be sold. It's imperative to look at the price and do what it does, lest we regret. Profitable trading goes hand in hand with positive expectancy, realities, normal psychology and risk management.

Conclusion

When it comes to successful trading, consensus opinions would hardly feed you and your family. If consensus opinions worked, then the majority would be winners. The modern market conditions don't usually favour buy-and-hold methodology; and where the markets are perpetually weak, you should simply sell short and rake in profits. There are many permanently successful financial institutions and there are ones that have gone kaput. The same is also true of private traders. There is no reason that you can't become successful through your speculative activities. We urge you to learn how accurate risk management can lead to peace of mind and happiness in the future.

This chapter ends with a quote from Simit Patel. It's all about taking small losses, so that your account can recover quickly when the markets become favourable.

"…Not every trade is going to be a winner, but so long as opportunities are taken and losses are kept small, this is not a problem. It is the big losses that are fatal, and it is the fear of taking trades that causes traders to miss the winners. Psychology is likely the biggest obstacle to success: taking small losses and bouncing back from them when setups appear is essential to success, and is the real reason success remains so elusive to so many."

Chapter 6: Whether I Win Or Lose A Trade...

NZD AUD

A Heart-to-Heart Talk

Experience is the best teacher. Negativity in trading is compared to temporary setbacks in real life: it exists so that you can become a better trader. Losing streaks are the equivalent of transient disappointments that celebrities face in their careers. They simply enable you to become an efficient risk manager. There are many life examples that can be compared to trading. Do you know that you need to be determined enough to surmount any challenges you might encounter in the markets? Uncertainty will forever be our source of wealth! Do you know that you need to believe in yourself? You're never doomed to failure in the markets. You just need to work hard enough until you reach the stage of trading effortlessly (after your past errors have turned you into a general of the financial markets). Can you do this? Do you agree with me? If you can, your dreams can ultimately be achieved.

"You can't change what you can't face and you can't face what you don't know." – Dr Woody Johnson

Whether I win or lose a trade, trading is my profession and it's what I like to do. Great people have always faced challenges and failures – yet they become great. The past failures and challenges in the markets are never a deterrent to me. Markets wizards today were novices in the past. The road to success is bumpy indeed. Nevertheless, the resplendent reward of consistent success makes the pain of the past pale into insignificance. Whenever I visualize the joy of success, the glory of breakthrough, the pleasure of financial freedom, the luxury of attainment of goals – the benefits in trading are worth the sacrifices inherent in it. I'll continue to move on.

Whether I win or I lose a trade, I'm still a trader and I'll be a trader for as long as I live. A balanced trading life doesn't preclude a normal person from having fun from other aspects of life. Trading is a holistic way of life: it's a journey to self-discovery. A successful trader is someone who has won one of the life's most crucial battles. Successful traders worldwide, I salute you! You're heroes and heroines indeed! You've discovered your true self. You've conquered your negative personality.

Whether I win or I lose a trade, I'll never quit. Losers and winners are a normal part of the game. I was downtrodden and hopeless on the markets in the past, but I experienced a turnaround once I got to know the tips and tricks for survival on the markets, and I'm disciplined enough to follow them. Yes, a trader may say he's surviving the markets instead of saying that he's successful. I was lucky to come across those with the right thoughts on the markets. For two real traders, there are ninety trading charlatans. There are too many crooks out there – too many wolves in sheep's clothing. But I can't be deceived anymore. I'm free from all their lies and marketing traps. I'm free!

"If you ever find yourself in the middle of a bumpy road in trading or in life, stay encouraged. You will make it to the peak if you realise that the valley is NOT your permanent address. Never forget, to become a butterfly, you must want to fly so badly that you are willing to give up being a caterpillar. Growth and change always go hand-in-hand with failure and fear. If you approach failure and challenges with a positive attitude, you will see how quickly you can use failure to achieve success." – Sam Seiden

Whether I win or lose a trade, I'm on my journey to trading mastery. Why wouldn't a warrior constantly pray for opportunities to show her or his prowess? I'm glad to be an experienced soldier on the battlefield of the financial markets. A soldier I am, yet I'm still learning. I'll be a learning soldier forever, for the market is a complex thing. Trading being the second most stress-related job in the world, second only to disarming live nuclear weapons, it can be approached with stress-reducing tactics. There are normal reactions to stress and these I know. Stress, just like risk, can be managed successfully.

Whether I win or lose a trade, I won't show any infantile reactions. I can be encouraged by a good trade, but I won't be discouraged by a bad trade. Some others may abandon this way of life, but I won't. People' negative thoughts and comments on trading aren't a headache to me. The outside world is very hard – harder than we may think. I'll let go of the past and look forward to a brighter tomorrow. Trading is my niche; I'm comfortable with it. If you invest the time in becoming an expert then the financial reward can be huge. I'll continue following the simple time-tested winning strategies. What benefits can you derive from an excellent speculation strategy if you fail to stick to it consistently irrespective of alternate winning and losing streaks?

Whether I win or I lose a trade, I'll be a successful trader. I'm just desperate enough for success (badly desperate) or I can say that those who've quit trading weren't desperate enough for success. I'm aware that nothing in the market is ever perfect; no Golden Goose method of making money. Nevertheless, I'd like to declare, without mincing words, that the probability of survival is strong if a positive expectancy speculation method is used regularly with self-control.

Whether I win or lose a trade, trading is an exciting world – a world of unlimited opportunities. Believe it or not, I'm moving up gradually higher and so you can. The me I see is the me I'll be. Welcome to the world of financial freedom.

Conclusion

This chapter concludes with a quote from Ken Long:

"(When it comes to trading mastery) You already have the mastery within you, waiting to be called forth... Mastery is walking the path, not the destination. Should you choose to walk it each and every day, what will you find?"

Chapter 7: Teach Your Teens the Art of Trading

GBP USD

"Children are very precious. Parents are also very caring. Do you know this?"

Most parents want the best for their children and they strive to achieve their aims, even in the face of stubborn obstacles and difficulties. A serious religious parent teaches their children about their faith when they're still very young. In fact, a famous proverb says: "Train a child in the way he should go and when he is old he will not turn from it." When an average child is asked, what do you want to be in life? The common answer is: "I want to be an engineer or a doctor or banker or a pilot or a lawyer or a footballer," etc. No-one will say, "I want to be an online trader." Why? It's because this is the mindset that is impressed into them by their folks, since they themselves are yet to grasp the potential of online trading. Those who know about it think it's too risky, without knowing the principles that can lead to everlasting victory in the markets.

Forex trading is one of the best vehicles that can be used to shield yourself from the persistent pecuniary uncertainties, widespread unemployment and sudden dismissals from jobs, which are so rampant nowadays. Many were having high aims when young, but now they've been disillusioned. The idea of going to school, studying hard to get good grades and then getting a good job, no longer always works. Why are there very few genius traders? It's because many people aren't exposed to the world of trading until they're very much older. If teens are exposed to trading on demos, as they practice risk-free on the virtual accounts that are subject to the real market data and conditions, their trading genius would be awakened. Wouldn't you want your child to be a trading genius before the age of 22? Would it be possible for anyone to be a genius in other fields of human endeavours if they're not yet a genius by the age of 22?

Teens should be taught the art of trading, but they should be restricted to demo accounts only, until they reach the legal age in which they can make independent financial decisions on their own. Yes, teens shouldn't open live accounts until they come of age. However, they can play with demo accounts (as if playing Nintendo games) until their skills are improved. In this regard, demo accounts are a unique tool in teaching your children. If a child is to become great in life, observant parents will notice some traces of greatness in the child while he or she is still young. Your children would learn by experience that uncomplicated methods of speculation ought to be used. If you really love trading and know that it can bring financial freedom (as it has done for countless known and unknown people), why can't you teach your children (especially your teens) how to trade? You can show them how to do this when they're on holidays or long vacations and encourage them to do further research on their own and practice their own ideas.

It's a pity that there are still many people who procrastinate. They don't know that what can be started today shouldn't be postponed till tomorrow. Some say: "I'm not yet settled down. Once I'm settled down, I'll start learning Forex." Others say: "There are some things I'm doing right now. Once I finish those things, I'll start learning trading." The fact is that there will always be things you're doing. So if you don't start learning, there'll always be alibis. The earlier one starts the journey to financial freedom, the better. The earlier you start learning about the markets, the earlier you attain the level of trading mastery. My regret is that I didn't start Forex trading earlier. If I'd started it far earlier, I'd have gone very far in attaining my trading goals and ambitions. But thankfully, I'm now in the race.

As for me, I'm going to teach my son on demos while he minds his formal education, I'll also teach him how to spend less than one hour per week on the markets and yet be a profitable trader. I want him to become a market wizard, becoming financially independent in future, unless he chooses otherwise (since I'm not going to force my opinions on him).

Jeff Cooper, when he was still young, learned the art of trading from his father, and he later became a legend of Wall Street. He had love for trading that kept him searching until he discovered the secret of permanent success. Mike Baghdady learned from his father, and has now become a blessing to the trading world. Peter Soodt learned from his father, and he's now a celebrated and profitable trader/coach. Joe Ross was taught by his uncle when he was just 14, and he's now one of the most experienced and the most eclectic traders in the world. He trades for a living and has insatiable passion for teaching how the markets work. Philipp Schroeder and Valentine Rossiwall are both young and highly profitable traders. Philipp and Valentine have other goals in mind, yet they take trading seriously. Oh, how bright and beautiful the future of these young men would be! Anton Kreil started trading while in his late teens and he retired from the investment banking industry at the age of 28. He now trades his own money and enjoys financial freedom, and he's still in his early 30s. Kenneth L. Fisher learned about trading from Philip Fisher, his father (who was a great investor) before he founded his own investment firm. He's on the 2011 Forbes 400 list of richest Americans. He was worth $1.7 billion in 2012. As of 2010, his company manages $41.3 billion in 38,521 customer accounts and has been called the largest wealth manager in the United States.

With time, your kids would be forced to be disciplined – in the face of negativity and uncertainties they face on demos. This really calls for rock-solid discipline, meaning that one needs to stick to one's time-tested trading plans. Negativity shouldn't be termed as stupidity, for that notion can't help their trading mindset. If they follow their trusted trading rules and they make profits on demos, they will be happy. It's joyous to see your efforts bringing great results realise and that your goals are being achieved.

Conclusion

The world needs traders – profitable traders. Can your child be one of them? Successful traders came from many areas and different walks of life. They have individual personalities, various strong points and weaknesses. As your kids have a feel for the markets, they'll forever remember their mistakes and a number of beautiful trades – a great experience that will pave the way for trading mastery. They'll quickly metamorphose into mature traders. Sharing trading facts with others bring us more satisfaction than keeping the secrets to ourselves.

This chapter ends with a quote from Louise Bedford:

"You see, studies have shown that those who believe that they can alter their behaviour and their habits to create a different outcome are happier people. They persist for longer. They score better on tests… Those who think they can't change, and that intelligence is fixed tend to quit at the first sign of trouble and don't stick around long enough to master a skill."

Chapter 8: Be Patient

EUR USD

Why aren't we patient while trading? Why do we always prefer instant results? Our culture has become one of immediate gratification, and we expect profits to come quickly and efficiently in the way we want.

When that doesn't happen, we tend to become increasingly frustrated and irritable – a sign of impatience. One source says that in trading, impatience is linked to frustration, irritation and even anger. Such emotions can raise our stress levels, which in turn can harm our health. Being impatient isn't just harmful in trading, it's also harmful in other areas of life. Author Marvin Lewis writes: *"In an act of impatience, a man in San Francisco, California, tried to beat traffic by swerving around a lane of cars that had come to a stop. However, the lane he pulled into had just been laid with fresh cement, and his Porsche 911 got stuck. The driver paid a high price for his impatience."* (Our Daily Bread, 19 February 2012).

Impatience Can Be Harmful

These are some of the adverse effects of impatience in trading.

1. *Dithering.* Impatience eventually leads to procrastination in making trading decisions, which is ironic. Could it be that some people feel compelled to postpone financially risky and highly competitive tasks of playing the markets, because they don't have the patience needed to work on themselves until they become an expert?

2. *Bad Trading Decisions.* Certain good strategies require patience before you can find the best setups. If you are impatient, you can make hasty trading decisions that violate your rules and later regret it. An impatient trader can make some unwise adjustments to open orders. Impatient speculators often make hurried, dismal speculation choices.

3. *Margin Calls.* The fate of most people in the financial markets is the consequence of undue impatience, coupled with inordinate avarice. Lack of patience in trading has led numerous traders to overleverage their portfolio excessively (instead of using high leverage judiciously) because they want to turn a small portfolio to a five-figure income as soon as possible. Newbies who make huge gains and huge losses are less happy than those who go for small losses and consequently small profits. The use of small position sizing and safe risk control doesn't appeal to those who want instant gratification. According to Clem Chambers, CEO of ADVFN, you should strive to get rich slowly rather than to get rich quickly. Looking for instant riches tends to satisfy human emotions, but it can lead to quick penury.

4. *Loss of Reputation.* No-one wants to be identified with failures. If you can keep your investors' portfolios safe, even in spite of small profits, you'll still be popular with them. But if you go after the biggest possible profits within the shortest possible time (this target is attainable, but rarely leads to everlasting success in the markets) and you happen to lose your investors' portfolios, you'll lose your reputation. Once your reputation is lost, it's extremely difficult to gain it back. It's better to be safe than to be sorry. Some gurus were popular yesterday, but because of impatience, they lost their reputation. I've always featured profitable generals of the markets and will still feature many more. However, I'm not interested in market wizards that crashed and got burned. I'm only interested in those that are permanently successful. These

successful traders have protracted periods of flat performances, followed by protracted periods of roll-downs, followed by protracted periods of consistent profits. The great thing about all these periods is that these generals of the markets remain patient throughout the successive periods and they survive the markets in the long run.

Stop Being Impatient!

It does little good to worry over things you can't control. The more patient you are in the markets, the more likely you are to have better results, make better decisions and progress in your career. Instead of losing patience over circumstances that are beyond your control, try to identify things you can control as a trader. For example, have a realistic view of trading. First of all, in reality, things don't often transpire as we want. Don't forget that you can't control everything that happens to you in life. Accept that time moves at the speed of time and not at the speed of your expectations. Accept that the markets cannot be forced to give you profits; you simply need to do the right things as a trader and profits will take care of themselves. That's patience. Study the secrets of market wizards and learn how you can trade less anxiously and more patiently. In time, patience will become a quality that comes naturally to you.

Conclusion

Most people would attain their goals in life if they learn from their initial errors and try never to repeat them again. With step by step assimilation of the realities of their chosen endeavours, they master their various careers. The problem is that, most persons don't apply the principles of success to their speculative activities. They approach trading with levity. They simply dash into trading and see it's not that easy. They may stay away from trading briefly, only to come back and experience the same results, repeatedly. During this experience, they still fail to use it as leverage to trading mastery. They can use that experience to become astute speculators. Can that be the best thing to do? We approach university studies and professional courses with utmost seriousness, persevering in spite of obstinate hurdles. We approach highly competitive sports and other forms of commercial activities with staunch determination and unflinching commitment. But we tend to approach trading with levity. Trading is a very serious profession which we should approach with staunch determination and unflinching commitment.

A quote from Richard Russell ends this chapter:

"And if no outstanding values are available, the wealthy investor waits. He can afford to wait. He has money coming in daily, weekly, monthly. The wealthy investor knows what he is looking for, and he doesn't mind waiting months or even years for his next investment (they call that patience)."

Chapter 9: What You Need to Know About Strategy Accuracy

CHF EUR

Do you know how top traders handle their positions? Schools encourage us to multi-task flawlessly. The more errors a student makes, the worse the marks awarded and therefore the less commendation. Mistakes are frowned on in the medical world, business world and the engineering world. Indeed, the willingness to be perfect in all fields of human endeavours is acknowledged – an inborn tendency.

The tendency to be perfect has made neophytes believe that good traders should never lose; or should rather have a 85%-95% success rate. They think they need to always win in order to make gains. After a losing streak, some swear never to trade again. The fact is that people will do things that increase their enjoyment and refrain from what tends to aggravate their pains. People try to escape negativity by failing to trade new signals, since – psychologically – it's thought that more loss is avoided if new signals are not traded. You need to do away with bad thinking that has an adverse effect on your trading. When you have a negative trade, try to find out why and how you could improve your trading. Do not dwell on your past bad experiences since this does not help you. You need to focus on more opportunities ahead of you and not be weighed down by past events.

Those who wish for perfection while speculating would be quick to truncate their winners because they don't want them to revert to negative territory. As a result of this, a trading system that has more than 70% success should be evaluated in the context of the mean equity curve and drawdowns. Someone with 95% accuracy can receive a margin call on his account, if his position sizes are too big, and no stops are used, or the stops are too wide and take profit zones are too tight. Someone with less than 33% accuracy can become a permanent victor in the markets, if his position sizes are very small, and he uses stops, and rides his winners or he sets tighter stops and wider take profit zones. You can win three trades, lose seven trades, lose another seven trades and win an additional two trades and still be a winner. Conversely, you can win eight trades, lose two trades, win another eight trades and lose an additional two trades and eventually receive a margin call. It all boils down to money management, golden rules of trading and risk control. Therefore, in spite of being inborn, perfectionism doesn't work in trading.

My long experience as a trader and trading systems developer shows that over a very long period of time, one would not be right for more than half of the time (if many signals are generated on monthly or yearly basis), even if it appears that one achieves 100% accuracy under certain market conditions. Very soon, a winning technique undergoes some losing streaks, whether on a monthly, quarterly or yearly basis. There aren't many speculators who can boast of more than 65% success in many years. These traders are geniuses and often apply common sense with any trading methodologies they use. There's not much psychological benefit from a winning trade that's realised when we violate our rules. That winning trade is only realised out of luck. We should accept the fact that we're the ones that opened a losing trade as well as a winning one. This is a fact.

Are market wizards (generals of the markets) achieving 90%-100 % success rates consistently? If we analyse their trading performances since the beginning of their various careers, we would see that this is far from being true. Think of Dr Brett N. Steenbarger, Dr Alexander Elder, Philip Fisher, David Harding, Adrian Manz, John Templeton, Michael Covel, Tim Knight, etc. These are successful names in the trading world, but they did not achieve 100% accuracy. While being right less than half of the time, they still achieved decent percentage returns. They simply make more money than they lose. You see, the market presents equal opportunities to everybody on earth. Everybody competes in the market, but only the skilful and the disciplined come out home and dry. How many percentage returns do you think Warren Buffet make on annual basis? Do you think he doubles his accounts every year? There are even years in which Warren doesn't make a profit at all. There are also traders who perform better than him, but they have smaller portfolios.

How could you end up winning with a lower hit rate? That will be explained in another chapter. Wasn't it 40% accuracy that gave me nearly 12,000 pips (49%) in 2011? Wasn't it only 35% accuracy that gave me 4,500 pips (21%) in 2012? Isn't it less than 40% accuracy that has given me over 2,200 pips (10.2%) so far in this year? Even with this, I usually have more than a few months of losses in a year. Sometimes, I even lose more than five or ten trades in a row, and yet I don't go down more than 5% or 8%. This is possible because of my very small lot sizes and risk control techniques. I know that I have got to cut my losers, or else I'm in trouble. I just ensure the losses are so small that whenever the market conditions become ok for me, I shoot ahead. For example, if I win ten or fifteen trades in a row, I gain about 10% or 16% or even more.

Conclusion

It's common that certain traders don't consider exotic pairs and crosses when they trade, because they're not as popular as majors and because their spreads aren't tight as those of majors. Should you trade on an instrument with a higher spread when the spread on the GBPUSD is much lower? Why would you trade the GBPCFH when the EURUSD is readily available? Some think that low spreads matter and that high spreads could magnify losses and reduce gains. This is true. But there are many wonderful opportunities on those exotic crosses as well, especially if you're using a trend-following strategy. If the GBPNZD moves by more than 500 pips in one week, would it matter much if the spread on it is 20 pips?

This chapter concludes with a quote from George Soros:

"I'm right in arguably no more than half of all cases, but I just make a lot of money whenever I'm right, and lose as little money as possible when I'm wrong."

Chapter 10: A Woman's Addiction To Forex

CAD CHF

Trading is Ideal for a Woman

Women can be, and are, great traders as well. They certainly have admirable qualities that can also help them in trading. There's no level of success in trading that isn't attainable by women. I foresee that the number of women in trading will increase geometrically.

The purpose of the interview you're about to read is to encourage women to come out of their comfort zone and embark on their journey towards real financial freedom. N. Hayes is just a woman like you (or your wife, mom, sister and aunt). But she's taken a noble decision – to be a successful trader. It's a wonderful privilege for me to present this interview with her to you. Here we go:

Azeez: Please introduce yourself.

N. Hayes: Hi everyone, my name is N. Hayes, but most people call me N. I am currently living in Europe and I have been trading forex for more than a year now. Before being a trader, I worked in the hospitality industry, in the Human Resources Department. I enjoyed it very much but I am definitely enjoying Forex more. Trading started out as just a hobby to pass the time and it has now become my full time job and I love it. Travelling is one of my favourite pastimes, other than reading, cooking, gardening, watching movies and TV series. Currently, I am looking at expanding my career by taking a full ten-month intense course in Money Management, Psychology of Trading, Forex Foundation, etc. My goal is to help others get started in trading and to share my knowledge and experience in this business.

Azeez: How did you start your trading career and what really motivated you to start trading?

N. Hayes: I quit my Human Resource Management job a little more than year ago and started trading full time. I have been hooked on trading since early last year when I had to spend so much time at the hospital and at home due to a shoulder injury. I was bored and started to surf around and I came across an informative website on Forex. Coming from a job with administrative and financial background, I became interested in Forex and I immediately opened an account (real account!) and started trading like a pro (no knowledge in FX at all except two years in the futures market many years back). I margined out my 2k account in less than a month! That didn't stop me from funding my account again. I promised myself that I would get my 2k back from the market. But this time, I subscribed to a signals provider and learn how to trade by reading FX websites, forums etc. I was doing well, my account tripled the amount and that was when I decided to be a full time FX trader and said goodbye to my well-paying job. I love the freedom of being able to work from home and the freedom to travel! My first Forex related holiday was to the Las Vegas Trader's Expo, last year in November, which I highly recommend to all traders, especially the ones who are new to this business and wanting to gain more knowledge in trading.

Azeez: Do you think women should be seriously encouraged to trade?

N. Hayes: Being a female trader, one must be prepared to accept her position as an outsider – trading is a man's world (I heard this often but I don't see it this way). This is definitely not gender specific. There are definitely more men in this business, but success and failure come from inside oneself. Of course, the circle of 'friends' will be more men than women, I can vouch for this. Having thicker skin helps because it does get brutal sometimes, especially when you are trading with a group, sharing ideas and learning from one another. It can get nasty! Anyway, if one's goal is to become a successful trader, then they need to do whatever it takes to learn a strategy, a method, practice it over and over again until it becomes second nature. You may need to work harder as a woman to prove yourself, but that is just a part of the excitement and challenge. Take the challenge and you will be successful. There are many free educational materials that you can download online and plenty of websites that offer great trading information. You just need to spend time searching for them. If it is tough to be learning on your own, then work with a trading coach or get a mentor to help you and to keep you growing as a trader. Do not be afraid to get help or ask! There are no right or wrong questions. I know some women are scared of sounding silly by asking a specific question. This fear is rather baseless in many respects. I believe it is time for more women to become traders. Contrary to what some might believe, trading does not turn a woman into becoming a non-feminine woman or developing a tough personality. Trading is a refreshing change to the female-dominated professions and I do know some women who choose to become a full trader, mainly because of the freedom it offers. A friend of mine who chose to be a full time trader is a great mom to her daughter. She made a deliberate decision to spend more time with her family and less time in the office. It was not an easy choice as she enjoyed her job very much but she realised that Forex can give her the freedom and flexibility of being a mom and a career woman. Being a trader, she does not need to be at the office eight hours a day.

Azeez: What do you think are the qualities peculiar to women that could help them in trading?

N. Hayes: I think the best qualities we women have is the ability to multi-task, use our intuition, and our perseverance. I also believe that our ability to separate our trading lives from our personal lives is a big bonus, as it helps to alleviate the stress of trading... we have other outlets to relieve our stress.

Azeez: What kind of trader are you? What is your style of trading?

N. Hayes: I used to be more of a scalper (very short term trader) but lately, since becoming a full-time trader, I am more of a day and swing trader now. This matches perfectly with my method of trading as my trades are based on technical analysis. I am quite conservative in choosing my trades, the ones with high probability set ups.

Azeez: How do you analyse the markets? What are your favourite pairs/crosses and timeframes?

N. Hayes: Being a conservative technical trader, I describe myself as practical, realistic and decisive when it comes to trading. I love facts and what I think is concrete. I have a set of standards (in my trading plan) and I follow them consistently. With rules in hand, I have no problems weighing alternatives and take rapid decisive action. I let my charts speak to me and I listen to them. I started with EURUSD and USDJPY but now I am trading most of the majors and the AUDJPY and USDJPY for crosses. For trade set ups, I start at the higher timeframes: daily, H4 and one hour. When executing and exiting trades, I will move to the lower timeframes, 30 minutes.

Azeez: Could you please tell us how you apply money management?

N. Hayes: Money management is so important, next to a trading plan and psychology of trading. You see, why most traders fail when they come to the market is they rely on their emotions to make their trading decisions. With good MM, I don't need to worry about my emotions while I am trading. I have in my trading plan how many pips I am willing to risk per trade and how many trades I have to make if I have few losses in a row etc. I cannot emphasize enough how important a trading plan is.

Do keep in mind that all big losses once began as small losses. Moreover, if you let a losing trade turn into a big loss, that's going to have a detrimental effect on your trading capital, and once you take a couple of big losses, it's much more difficult to trade and to gain back the money which you've lost. These mistakes can be easily prevented if you have a good money management.

How do I determine how much money I actually make on a particular trade? Well, it depends on how much money I actually put into the trade. My usual ratio is 2:1 and 3:1 (low and high probability trades)

Azeez: I really appreciate your blog (http://www.smurfette4x.com/). What are the aims behind this blog?

N. Hayes: The aim behind my blog is to help other traders that are just entering the trading world. My goal is to share the knowledge I have gained with everyone in an attempt to make it less intimidating for people considering trading.

Azeez: Do you fancy or at least, would advise the use of trading robots?

N. Hayes: These so called 'Expert advisors' have their pros and cons. I do believe that some work but again a trader needs to spend some time looking for the right one. Also, the mentality of the trader plays an important role in this. There is no such thing as earning money without doing any kind of work. Many people get themselves burned by ignoring the fact that research and testing are definitely a must before they link these Expert Advisors to their live account. Learn how these Expert Advisors work first before having your hard earned money totally at the mercy of a program. There is no doubt of the high success rates that these systems hold but while these values are very positive, it is important to realise the risk that accompanies these rates of success. These experts are programs for certain market conditions and not for difficult market conditions that could lead to serious losses. As for myself, I am currently testing an Expert Advisor which is programmed based on the Grid Trading technique and so far, I am quite happy with it. (Grid Trading is a trading technique that uses a series of pending orders creating a 'grid'.)

Azeez: Everyone has their strengths and weaknesses, what do you think is your greatest strength and your weakness as a trader?

N. Hayes: I think my strength is that I'm willing to put as much energy and focus into the job as I have to. My greatest weakness would be that I become a little more cautious and doubt my instincts when I have multiple losses, but on the positive side I don't give up and work towards improving my skills no matter what.

Azeez: How many pips on average, do you make per month?

N. Hayes: I have a daily goal of 20-50 pips. Monthly average is between 500-1,000, it really varies, depending on the market. Also, I am more of a conservative trader; I would rather wait for the market to give me a trade than jumping in just for the sake of making some pips. There are times that I don't trade for a few days, when I don't see any good, solid setups. It is fine with me. Since becoming a full time trader, I realise how much it pays to be patient and disciplined.

Azeez: What do you enjoy doing apart from trading?

N. Hayes: Traveling! My favourite destination is the USA. This is one of the reasons why I decided to be a full-time trader, I can work from anywhere in the world, as long as I have my laptop with me.

Azeez: Do you have any advice for traders out there, especially female traders like you?

N. Hayes: I am not sure if I am the right person to give out any great advice here as I am still 'learning' myself. This is the best part of this business, one never stops learning. There is always something new and the market doesn't pause for us. We need to keep updated and try not to fall too far behind. One reminder that I apply to myself and I would like to share with others, is that "If you are satisfied with the kind of work you're doing and why you are doing it, you will be successful." I really believe in this. If you put your heart in it and are willing to learn as much as you possibly can, you will open up doors you can't even imagine. Never let others influence you otherwise, because if you let others define what success is for you… then it is pretty easy to stray and to lose sight of yourself. Everyone has their own dreams and goals, never forget that. Also, don't let fear get in the way. Trading is ideal for a woman. It takes time to master so one has to have patience in order to be able to succeed in this business. This is a profession that takes a lot of hard work, focus, strength (emotionally) and determination but if you have what it takes and if you are up for the challenge, you can do it!

Azeez: What are your plans for the future, as far as trading is concerned?

N. Hayes: I am described by friends as a flexible person. Not to mention a daring one. I do have plans for my future but my plans are mostly adjustable. I go with the flow. I prefer to tell you about my dreams instead, as they are more concrete and something that I am really looking forward to and working on. My dream is to be among the successful women in this line of business some day, with a good trading portfolio. My trading blog is a start, for me to share my ideas with my followers. I want to expand from here, maybe giving lessons in a subject that is related to trading. My aim is to help new traders in realizing the reality of what Forex can give them and not seeing it behind rosy glasses. In short I would like to help prevent others from making the same mistakes that I have made in the beginning of my career.

Azeez: N. Hayes, thank you very, very much for this insightful interview!

Chapter 11: Conflicting Opinions in Trading

JPY CAD

The trading world is full of too many different ideas that are hyped excessively. Many a professional often asserts that their own trading idea is the best.

Many traders breathe intraday trading, and many endorse investing. Some worship tape reading, while some idolize Fibonacci ratios. Some use supply and demand levels in trading, and some simply scalp. Some espouse chart patterns with Elliot waves, while some use indicators. Certain traders do trend-following only, while other traders have adopted contrarian trading methods. Trading performances of dedicated chart analysts and dedicated news analysts have been showcased, but each group attempt to disparage the kind of analysis adopted by the opposite group, which has been triumphant. Some say the use of stops is mandatory; some say they're successful without stops.

The list can be endless...

As Dr Van K Tharp has always put it, people trade their beliefs, not the markets. Dr Tharp trades according to his beliefs. I trade according to my beliefs, and you trade according to what you believe. What's useful for you may not be useful for others. If you use something successfully and you're happy with it, others may not use it successfully. The reason why is because that thing doesn't fit them. If you disagree with others, you may want to assert that your opinions are superior. What you disagree on may not be useful to you. If you argue that your opinion is the best: remember that many others would always use logical reasoning to underline what they believe and make what others believe appear useless.

The Best Trading Ideas

Experiencing a losing trade or a positive trade turned negative often results in feelings of pain, anger and frustration. Are you in the midst of a discouraging situation? Remember that the markets have immense riches in them. Keep this fact in the forefront of your mind; remind yourself of it repeatedly in your career. Why we may not understand why some market circumstances seem unfair to us at times, we understand that we can still be permanently triumphant in the market.

I know this from personal experience. After I've accepted the truth about trading, my experience in the markets has become smoother and better. That's not to say that I never have losses in trading after this, but every loss is faced with the knowledge that I'm using a positive expectancy system. I never feel sorry I started trading, and I still love the profession today. My only desire is to keep my portfolios safe in face of permanent uncertainties in the markets. I never feel any desire to back down regarding trading.

In the trading world today, the quest for great profits can lead in many directions, but only those who focus on how to control risk and DD will be truly triumphant in the markets. Some contrarian techniques even allow positivity consistently.

Then what is the best trading idea? Jack D. Schwager's latest book is called *Market Sense and Nonsense*. Ok, this means that there are senseless and sensible ideas in the markets. Good trading ideas allow you to risk far less than you aim to gain. These ideas let you know when to enter the market and when to stay out of the market. They give you some effective risk control rules. Good trading ideas won't let you sustain big losses during unfavourable market conditions. Sensible trading ideas will make you victorious in the long run. With these kinds of ideas, you can't avoid losses, but you're sure to make more money than you lose ultimately.

Note: Any trading ideas that can't achieve the objectives in the paragraph above are useless ideas, no matter how popular they are. Any trading idea is useful only if its balance increases over a long period of time, or there are gains to make at the end of a specified trading period.

Conclusion

Trading isn't always easy, but the results of commitment to trading success will be evident in your career. You shouldn't expect to get an emotional uplift or feeling of quiet peace every time you trade, but as you continue your commitment, your attitude, outlook and conduct will be like those of matured traders who are called market wizards. Speculation is full of challenges, but we can overcome them all.

This chapter ends with the quote below:

"The best theory doesn't do you any good unless it works in the real world." – Larry Connors

Chapter 12: How Much Is Needed To Open A Forex Trading Account?

NZD JPY

In one of his past articles, the world-famous Dr Van K Tharp stresses one of the most important reasons why most people find it very difficult to make money in the markets: that most people don't have enough money.

Too many people open accounts with too little money, so they can't execute proper money management, neither can they expect to live on small accounts.

You can open a Forex account with $1; you can also open it with $50 billion. While most brokers have minimum deposits limit, they've no maximum deposits limit. Some brokers even offer micro or mini and/or cent accounts so that traders with small money can trade while having many options to control risk. Happily, gone are the days when traders needed huge amounts of money to capitalize on market opportunities. Nowadays, high leverage allows you to make larger transactions with smaller capital. High leverage is a curse to those who are ignorant of sound position sizing and risk control, while it's a blessing to those who are aware of that.

The bigger your capital, the bigger your returns, and the smaller your capital, the smaller your returns. Let's assume trader A opens an account with $1,000, trader B opens an account with $10,000 and trader C opens an account with $100,000. If traders A, B and C make

20% each on their respective accounts on an annual basis, here's their personal income in that year.

Trader A makes $200. Trader B makes $2,000, whereas Trader C makes $20,000. You see, hedge fund managers make millions or billions of dollars as profits because they invest millions and billions of dollars.

As you probably know, your account must be big before you can make good profits (for a small percentage gain would make a huge difference). You can open an account with small money; say $50 or $250 or $500. However, don't expect to make a living from such small capital. Personally, I believe that if you want to make a living from trading, your account should not be less than $20,000. This would give you an excellent position sizing and risk control flexibility.

For you to make a living from $1,000 or $5,000 or $10,000, you need higher risk, which also comes with a possibility of a worrisome roll-down. With $100 or $300 or $500, one can experience the thrill of speculation, but one must never expect to make a living from that. Those who want to make a living from an account that small would need to double the account many times. Do you know what that is? It's called suicide trading. This is because what can double your account also has the potential to result in big losses or a margin call.

If you would like to open a big account but your financial circumstances preclude you from doing that, you can still open a small account and begin to trade. Just don't expect big profits from a small account; which means that you need to be realistic and lower your expectations. As long as you have other sources of income, you should be fine, and there shouldn't be any pressure on you to double your account quickly.

Conclusion

You can start trading with a very small account, but that one has fewer merits than a big account. Evidently, you need big accounts to trade safely and make decent profits. As you trade, you shouldn't forget to have entry and exit points in mind. Great speculators have an exit target for each of their positions, whether the position ends in a positive zone or a negative zone. Then don't risk too much per trade. Risking less per trade would surely give you good profits as you also have the ability to curtail losses so that they don't have a big impact on your portfolio. Long-term survival in the trading world means that your past errors have taught you to become a better trader.

The quote below is taken from Dr Chris Kacher. It shows that it isn't correct to say that one can't enjoy lasting success in the markets.

"I realised the efficient market theory was not relevant in the real world when it came to developing a sound strategy that put the odds in its favour. In the long run, statistics always win, and is why the house in gambling casinos always comes out ahead." (Source: Tradersonline-mag.com)

Chapter 13: You Need a Trading Track Record

AUDNZD

A good trading track record is a noble achievement to aspire to. It's a proof of your trading prowess – an absolute requirement that must be provided before you're viewed as a pro, whose trading strategy is worthy of emulation or who could possibly be considered as a money manager.

Maintaining a consistent track record isn't something that's easily achieved, particularly in the face of the vagaries of the markets, but it's absolutely possible. A typical account history would have losing trades and winning trades; with average losses that are much lower than average profits. This account would surely have occasional roll-downs, which would now and then be recovered, provided the trader is using a positive expectancy system. Therefore a good account history is the one which survives all the odds of negative trades and drawdowns over a long period of time. The account history thus would have a current balance that's higher than the initial deposit, no matter how small or big the percentage profit is.

It's recommended by certain trading strategists that a trading system ought to be tested for at least four months on live market conditions. If the strategy then enables the account to be in a plus zone after the four-month period, then one could use it on one's account, with the premise that it would survive the future uncertainties if its rules are faithfully adhered to. That kind of strategy must enable the user to open long and short trades. One expert of trading track records declares that an account history must be, at least, two years old before the strategy/strategies used on it could be judged as being time-honoured and having any chance to survive the future uncertainties.

Mark Jurik, a celebrated trading maverick, once said that no strategy should be considered as being fit to be published unless a minimum of 500 trades have been placed with it. He also went ahead to state that such a strategy shouldn't be considered as being fit to be used in managing funds unless a minimum of 1,000 trades have been placed with it. If an account history is still in a plus zone after this, then the strategy used on it is really worth being considered.

One thing must be born in mind though; you don't need to double your account several times before you can be seen as a pro. During the bear markets of 2008, many fund managers ended the year with mild or severe roll-downs, and yet there was someone who ended the year with only 1% profit. With some shallow thought, one may think that's far from being impressive, but the real fact is that the person was able to avoid an annual roll-down. This means he was able to keep the portfolio he managed safe. The most important thing is the existence of your portfolio, not the profits made on it.

Build a track record, for it's an absolute essential. A typical investment bank might consider you for a fund manager position if you'd been trading on your own account for three years with annual profits of around 30%. You trading track records would, undoubtedly, open new doors for you. Go to various trading forums, blogs and websites, you'll see many participants who know lots of things about trading. These people live and breathe trading, yet the only people to be respected are those who have good track records. There are many people who do the talking, but they don't do the doing. Therefore, we respect only those who do the doing and do so successfully.

Having a good track record could make you wealthy, since many people may approach you with offers. There are renowned pros out there. Why do you think they're renowned? They have good track records. Dan J. Zanger, Peter Milman, Dr Brett N. Steenbarger and so on, have track records. Billionaire and millionaires traders have, in most cases, made their money from their investors. They're able to do this because they have track records. In the trading world, the most important qualification on the battlefield of the financial markets is your track record, not your PhD.

Conclusion

You shouldn't find an alibi for not having a track record after many years of trading. And this is achieved by giving your winners some leeway, as you truncate your losers. Negative positions must be closed. You see, the journey towards financial freedom is no picnic. In reality, it's ups and downs in all aspects, especially if you don't know the secrets to permanent success in the markets. No wonder only 10% enjoy everlasting success in the markets. You'll often go through periods of losing streaks and wrong trades, to the extent that, unless you're highly determined, you'll get fed up with trading and throw in the towel. If your goal is to get rich quickly, and you don't get rich as fast as you want, you'll decamp and join those who have stopped trading. Rather, your goal should be to get rich slowly: a record of 15% to 25% per annum is even a commendable achievement.

I'd like to conclude the chapter with the quote below:

"Expectancy (and statistics, for that matter) proves that cutting losers and maxing winners will eventually work out to be consistently (but not always) profitable." – Dirk Vandycke

Chapter 14: Why Small Position Sizes Are Ideal

USD EUR

Size Isn't Everything...

There are happy traders who say these things:

"The markets aren't hunting for me. I'm part of a large trading community. I know that losses are a normal part of doing any business. My winnings are on the way."

"I know that the volatility in the markets is normal. It's what has brought me gains."

"Trading has become my calling! I trade with peace of mind because my losses are small and easily recoverable."

I'm totally satisfied with whatever the markets give me – whether more or less. I just need to focus on risk control. Profits will take care of themselves.

Sadly, there are also suicide traders who say these:

"That's me, always perspiring profusely in this severe winter, and that's whenever there's a small movement against me."

"Why does the market always move against me? Who's my enemy out there? Contend, O Lord, with those who contend with me; fight against those who fight against me."

"The fluctuations of the markets are fluctuating my heart!"

"Can you see? Another loss. That's enough. I can't continue like this. I can't take it anymore."

If I use 0.01 lots per trade on a small account and make 500 pips in one month, my profits would be about $50 (whereas it would be $500 if I use 0.1 lots). Someone who uses 1.0 lot per trade would have made approximately $5,000 from a gain of 500 pips. 10.0 lots would have then brought approximately $50,000 as a profit. I'm not saying that I can't use big lot sizes, but it will be on sizable accounts, not relatively smaller accounts. Recently, someone in Russia made 3,500% profit in less than one week! Isn't that attractive? Isn't it a most welcome opportunity if you can increase your account 35 times in a week? We can see that higher risk enables us to make more money, but the demerit is that it can also bring huge losses when a trading strategy enters a protracted losing streak. Only small sizes can make one survive that kind of protracted losing streak.

For many years, I've always advocated the use of very small lot sizes when trading. This is mandatory for keeping one's portfolios safe permanently. Nevertheless, I've been derided for using minuscule sizes. Those who recommend big lot sizes won't ever tell you how many accounts they've blown. They may have more experience than me and have better strategies than I have. Yet, when it comes to risk management, I believe I've improved a lot. There were great traders in the past who are no longer trading. Why? They often bet too big in the markets that couldn't be predicted with absolute assurance. If you can't sleep because of open trades, if you can't leave your PC screen or you're crying or extremely anxious, then what you've risked is too high.

When negativity is considered against positivity, it's common for people to double or treble their risk after taking a loss, so as to recover quickly. Many traders feel that the bigger their position sizes, the bigger their profits. This mindset is wrong. The factors that can help grow your portfolios over time are conservative risk control, discipline and small lot sizes. Certain people feel that smaller position sizes are tantamount to smaller stakes, which reduce their income. Do you also want to use the RSI to build your new estate? There's an illusion of having huge gains when fat lot sizes are opened, though the real uncertainty comes from the inability to ride your positions for as long as possible, even with clear negativity. In addition, we go against the norm when we think the only way to control risk is to cut our profits quickly. Still, an effective speculative strategy can receive a margin call if position sizes are too large.

Stop losses must also be physical and rigid. We surmise that there are new trading setups which always come up every day. There are always new opportunities in the markets. As it always will be with small sizes, trades that hit stops would merely bring small, and therefore bearable, losses; and this is the usual way to push a portfolio from the recent drawdown to the eventual increase. It's the anticipated increase that overrides the recent drawdown. My personal positions sizing ideas aren't the most commonly accepted, yet I've always remained triumphant, no matter what the market does. The ideas that make you triumphant irrespective of what the markets do are great ideas.

We're not robots with no emotions, yet we tend to master irrational emotions as we gain more experience in the markets. When you risk too much, you'll attach excessive importance to every open position no matter what – so you need to change this attitude. The art of speculation should be approached with some form of rationality; it's not your whole world, for there are other things in life that matters a lot, so every open position is not your life. When you keep your lot sizes very small, and they don't eat your account with small unfavourable fluctuations, you're fine. When those lot sizes are very small and perpetual and loss trades don't make you cry, that's when you'll be able to control your emotions. Approach everything with rationality, treat each trade with a degree of sanity and cut how much you risk drastically if you're going gaga. Once again, drastically cut how much you risk and be responsible for that. Put a limit on how much you risk per trade, put a limit on how much your risk is per day or per week or per month. When you do this, then you know your maximum loss in a given period and you'll be satisfied with whatever the markets do to you. Yes, you'll be OK.

Great traders know that those who often bet big are suicide traders.

This chapter concludes with the insightful quote below:

"Do not risk more than 0.5 to one per cent of your capital per trade at the beginning. Less is often more. If you are used to the strategy and you have traded it over a longer period of time you can vary the risk and maybe even increase it. But you have to take the drawdowns of the strategy into account which increase with the higher risk. Be aware of your total risk: It is the sum of the open risk of all active positions. Your total risk should not be greater than 2.5 to five per cent – then your capital will not decrease too much if you have several losing trades." – Julian Komar (Source: www.tradersonline-mag.com)

Chapter 15: Who Should Be Your Trading Mentor?

CHF GBP

Experienced trading mentors have groomed successful traders over the years. While some frown on the idea of mentioning mentors, it's necessary to say that the writer of this book would have quit the trading world many years ago when things became so hopeless in the markets, if he hadn't come across those seasoned coaches and traders who revealed the secrets of successful trading to him.

It's reckless to assume that you can just read a few articles from some 'Golden Goose proponents' and then conclude that you can go to the battlefield of the financial markets on your own. The reality is totally different from this.

While it's possible to become successful after many trials and errors of your own, things will be very much easier and far less intricate if you go to the battlefield with a trading veteran who's also a talented trainer. It's easier for one to call oneself a hero/heroine before one faces a real battle. Those who ignore the fact above will eventually be forced to look for help when they face the quirk of the markets with their shallow experience.

You tend to be like trading mentors you like. They can be successful traders – or losing traders – based on whom you like. There are mentors whose trading principles are worth emulating. You don't need to have met the mentors face-to-face. In this internet age you and your mentor can telecommute.

Your trading mentor doesn't have to be perfect, nor always winning. It's unrealistic to think that a mentor must be a saint that no one can ever find any fault with. You also have your own weakness and human flaw. No human being is perfect and as such your mentors may exhibit some human errors, yet they would be exemplary when it comes to trading and some other professional aspects, and therefore they can be great role models in the world of trading.

It's possible that you have many trading mentors; as many as you want. One might be good at trading with precision accuracy, while another might be a good trading money and risk manager. Another one might be an expert in trading psychology and disciplined mindset. My own role models are many. They include Joe Ross, Dr Van K Tharp, Sam Evans, Dr Alexander Elder, Dr Emilio Tomasini, Loiuse Bedford and others.

How You Can Benefit from Your Trading Mentors

1. Carry out research and observe them and have an insight into their trading principles.

2. Interact with them. There are many technological devices that can be used in achieving this, like telephone, webinars, trading rooms, teleconferencing, chatting facilities, etc.

3. Ponder your role models' trading qualities, strengths and principles. As you ponder these, you can see yourself imitating them.

4. When you choose a trading mentor, your aim won't be to transform yourself to be exactly like the person. Probably, you still possess your own innate good trading traits and strengths.

Nonetheless, having role models in the trading world would help bring out the best in you as a trader.

You can learn as part of a trading team or group. Before you can become part of a hedge fund, you'll first need a good account history, even if your capital is small. Getting employed as a fund manager is highly dependent on your track records. Should you become part of a trading group, you would then need to gain more ideas from the most talented and the most proficient speculators in that group. Good reputation in trading has to do with your records and longevity – these are mandatory.

Excerpts from Trading Role Models

Quotes are beneficial and inspirational, for they have transformed many souls. Quotes from famous, seasoned and profitable traders are thus no exception. Below are excerpts from articles written by a few of my role models:

"People act like they've got all the time in the world, oblivious to the fact that the hourglass is running out of sand. They waste time when they could educate themselves. They entertain when they should focus…. People's lives seem to be getting more and more crammed with a lot of ignorance, self-entertainment one way or another, and… well… not much else. Don't let this world-wide trend define THIS month for YOU! You have a choice. Invest your time and reap the benefits. Spend your time and it will be gone forever." – Louise Bedford (Source: www.tradingsecrets.com.au)

"Learning to trade is different from learning to ride a bike; it's more like learning a profession. Unfortunately, most traders think they can just close their eyes, pick stocks, sit back and let the money roll in. But it doesn't happen that way, and eventually, new traders figure that out–often painfully. Successful trading takes a tremendous amount of planning, skill and training–just like any business venture. Essentially, your trading should be viewed as a business–because it is a business. And if you want that business to be profitable, you need to understand the parts

of your business, you need a good plan, and you need the discipline to follow the plan… If you're looking for a quick and easy way to make money in the markets, even Tharp Think won't help. There is no "silver bullet solution" to trading success." – Dr Van K Tharp (Source: www.vantharp.com)

Chapter 16: Angry Traders and Investors

EUR GBP

"If you are driven by the stock price you are going to go crazy." – **Michael Bigger**

There's no speculator in the world that hasn't, at some time or other in their career, experienced the emotion of anger. Every trader becomes angry because of some reasons. Even the renowned Dr Van K Tharp (a trading specialist) was once trading in an angry mood. Then, he was losing and he became angry. The more he lost, the angrier he became and the more he lost.

Trading is hard enough. So any factor that makes the matter worse – whether internal or external – would only add to our livid state of mind. For many traders, it's because of negativity they sustain now and then. Traders and investors are angry and you can see that in their comments, actions and trading results.

"What is my broker doing to me? Yes, the loss is becoming bigger and bigger. The account is going down. That fundamental analyst is an asshole! The website that recommended these shares as a sell opportunity has clearly misled me. They don't know what they're doing. Don't they know that the trend on the chart is up, the MACD signal lines and histogram are above the zero line and the Parabolic SAR is below the price? What are the Fibonacci ratios doing? Why couldn't they use Andrew's Pitchfork? Albeit, most renowned chart analysts also thought the shares would plummet. Why does the market always have me in mind so as to ruin me?"

Nevertheless, does anyone care? Culpable souls, events and situations are no longer a curiosity. Are they? You blame our leaders and politicians. You criticize anything or anybody that falls short of your standards or expectations. You deprecate positions that aren't going in your favour. You are quick to judge everything around you. Signals strategists, brokers, North Korea, the euro's unpredictability, Mark Carney, technical experts, software vendors, cliques, trade shows, central banks, interest rates, earthquakes, cyclones, harsh winters, the unrest in the Middle East, unemployment rate, power failure (you also want to sue your internet service providers), global warming, stock tipsters, TV media, tape readers, assassins, nuclear holocaust and hypocritical religions. You condemn your cruel manager, selfish chairman, CTAs, CFOs, UFOs, scalpers, high frequency trading, position traders, your fellow traders, insider traders, the bulls, bots manufacturers, drug dealers, street thugs, traffic jam/noises, racism, unfulfilled promises, unequal opportunities, bleak future, headache, sky-high commodity prices, Cuba, Syria and Central Africa. You deprecate your printer, your pet, the incompetent cook, harsh tax laws, police surveillance, your irritatingly haughty neighbours and your unforgiving spouse. Your favourite team lost their match. Your kid is a nuisance; and the list goes on. You are frustrated with everything.

"I know what I'm doing. It's those skunks that are insane. This thing has made me vulnerable; I can't control what the price is doing to me, for I'm just looking at the screen helplessly. My situation is hopeless – a prey of those institutional speculators. Why is Smart Money after me? Why do they want to ruin me? Why are they so bold? But I made the right decision before I sold the shares!"

Can this approach help you?

You're blindly furious, you punch your iPad, bang the door, break the dish, swear oaths loudly, scream at a skunk, threaten the security guard, or drink yourself into stupor. You're totally helpless. You can't be helped until you see yourself as the source of your trading problem and the source of your solution. You create the trading results you get. Stop blaming others and put the blame on yourself; otherwise, you can't find any solution. If it's going to be, it's up to you. The things, countries and the people mentioned above (plus anything/anybody you might have condemned), didn't place your trade for you. You made your own trading decisions and you should accept the outcome.

You can decide to buy, sell or remain neutral – irrespective of what experts or automated signals are saying. No-one forces you to take a position against your wish. You think it and come up with a resolution. If you make gains from your trading, who do you praise? According to the quote above, those who watch the prices every minute are going to go crazy. It pays to focus on the big picture and stick to your safety rules in trading. Day trading is full of stress and you're bound to get offended by the markets. You can't enjoy profits without experiencing the bitterness of losses. Sane traders know how to accept profits and losses with calmness of the mind, no matter how long a losing or a winning streak is. They just keep on managing their positions and controlling their losses. For those who passed out of school with good grades, achieve enviable results in other areas of human endeavours, collect pay checks regularly etc., it's not easy to accept loss in trading. They prefer 100% hit rate if possible. They don't want to think that they can still survive in the market with only 33.3% hit rate.

R. J. Hixson says that trading in an angry or depressed state can be as dangerous to your equity as trading in an ecstatic state. Anger can't improve any statistics in anything, as far as your trading career is concerned. The angrier you are, the more blunders you will commit, which you'll eventually regret. Make sure that you speculate on the trends you can comprehend and the markets you prefer. Even if your stops are hit after that, it's your decision. Don't add to your losers!

Conclusion

Instead of deprecating your adverse lot as a trader, you can trade successfully. This is the good news. Help is available. You just need to develop deep love for the markets and fuel your passion for successful trading principles by talking and sharing it again and again. Talk and discuss trading and its potential. Discuss with people of like passion… Don't spend time on wrong information that could dissipate your zeal; don't get discouraged by those who have no passion trading.

This chapter concludes with the quote below:

"It's difficult to trade with a peak performance mindset when you're in a bad mood. The more you can control your emotions, the more likely you are to maintain a winning edge." – Joe Ross

Chapter 17: Dedicate Yourself to Trading Success

USD CAD

"Trade as professionally as you can." – Mebane Faber

Successful trading is possible, but it requires dedication. You need to commit yourself to learning how to be the best trader you can be. Commit yourself to learning risk control and sound money management methods. Commit yourself to learning how to trade with peace of mind, irrespective of the market conditions. For you to make profits personally, you need to invest your time and money. Without this it's impossible to make profits. Trading always costs something.

As you probably agree, and based on your experience, making money in the markets is sometimes easy and it's sometimes difficult. When things are hard, dedicated traders minimize their losses and gain an insight that makes them become better traders. When things are easy, dedicated traders know that it's normal and expected. It's novices that are extremely joyous when things are easy, only to give up when things become hard.

Many times we look back for a few years on what we thought of as a flop and we see that our determination was leading us step by step. We may not have jumped from 'beginning' to 'end' in one attempt, but our determination was pushing us ahead. The wrong steps we took during our formative years in trading weren't a curse – they were blessings!

We would like you to benefit from trading. We're seriously interested in helping others to be the best traders they can be. We want you to be happy as a trader. You would have to stop the trading styles that don't help your account and seek winning standards that ensure permanent victory. The decisions you make right now will definitely affect your future career. It's better to make small profits and losses and be happy than make big profits and losses and end up being miserable. You can speculate consistently in the markets with peace of mind, knowing that your risk is always under control.

We want you to walk in the paths that lead to trading success, especially those that ensure permanent success. We want you to improve yourself. We want you to experience peace and happiness in your trading career – permanently. Do you want to live in the world of triumphant traders? Our regular contact with fellow experts strengthens our heart and determination to be successful. We too appreciate the notes and lessons we receive from experts. Don't keep this message to yourself. Share it with others as soon as you can!

This chapter concludes with the quote below:

"Realise that it can take a long time to become a successful trader, just as it can take long to become successful in any other business. You need time to build your trading skills. You need time to acquire experience in the market. Experience and skill ensure that, over the long term, you will become consistently profitable." – Joe Ross (Source: Trade2win.com)

Chapter 18: The Dark Side of the Corporate World

GBP CAD

"Let's face facts. Traders with huge trading fortunes only exist because they started doing small things. Once they got the little things right – they catapulted towards success." – Caroline Stephen

Some decades ago, many people went to school to get knowledge. But nowadays, most people go to school so that they can get jobs when they graduate. Many people crave the white collar job in the corporate world – otherwise known as the rat race. One dictionary describes the rat race as 'an exhausting routine that leaves no time for relaxation.' Is that want you want? Please read a true life story below.

One high school student invested profitably in a market and tasted the pleasure of trading. He later went to a university and got a degree that was an equivalent of MBA. He was lucky enough to get a job at IBM and began to play the corporate game. While he was still relatively young, he had gone very high on the corporate ladder. The career was successful: he flew across the world and rode in posh cars while on official assignments. He thought his own life was OK and that he would retire wealthy.

In the midst of the apparent ostentation, the man felt like a slave. He was working from Monday to Saturday and for up to 12 hours per day. He seldom went home and if he did, he had just a few hours to rest. He got no time for himself and other important things in life – not to mention friends. He began to experience the dark side of the corporate world.

From the Corporate Job to the Real Financial Freedom

From 2000 things began to move from bad to worse, with increasing targets and shrinking income. IBM merged with another company and several thousands of jobs were cut. The economic outlook got bleak and many companies laid off their workers. If he waited any longer, he might also be laid off; and it was better to resign than to get retrenched. The man quickly made up his mind to go back to trading. He tendered his letter of resignation and quit the corporate world.

He wasn't sure whether he would make it as a trader or not. He just wanted to give it a try. After all, he had enough money to survive for one year. He drastically changed his lifestyle and cut back his spending. He then left Germany and settled in the US. He purchased many trading courses and systems, but they didn't work for him. However, with some of the systems, he'd make money and then lose again. The forlorn man was moving towards the brink of penury.

On day, a trader friend invited him to a bar. They began to talk about trading and he told his friend that he was tired of losing. His friend didn't give him a strategy: he simply gave him a trading idea. That idea suddenly revolutionized his trading career. He tested it and saw that it worked best for him.

The man became so successful that he now lives a free and affluent life (a true hallmark of financial freedom). The man now lives in a very beautiful huge mansion on Lake Travis in Austin, Texas. His compound is very big and there is large swimming pool in it. His children are enjoying their dad's wealth and life's been really good to them.

Do you learn anything from this story? The name of the man is Markus Heitkoetter.*

The Best Job in the World

As you probably know, trading is the best job in the world. The best job, ironically, is also one of the most challenging. There's no successful trader today who didn't face challenges in the past. If you give up trading, you'll have no testimony or encouragement you can give others. If you keep at it, you'll soon attain your financial goals. You may not be very wealthy, but you'll be financially comfortable.

When starting out, it's essential to ensure that your mistakes don't have significant effects on you. It's not possible for noobs to make permanent success right from the start, for there are lessons to make from one's mistakes (which also involve pecuniary loss). You'll also make some wise decisions as a noob; plus you'll need to learn valuable lessons from all this. This is how you become a great trader eventually. The trading principles that worked more than a century ago can still work in today's markets.

Conclusion

Personally, I can now better control the effect of negativity on my accounts. I know that I've no ability to force the markets to move in my favour, but I can control my approach to the markets. This reality has been mentioned in my past articles. When I constantly retain my sanity – even in the face of losing trades – I'll not forget that I've been faithful to my entry criteria and I'll be looking forward to new trading setups. We have absolute control of our reactions to the outcome of our trades. That's what we need to do to keep on winning.

This chapter ends with a quote from Markus:

"I am fortunate to be friends with some of the most famous traders in the world. Sometimes we meet in Las Vegas, Chicago or New York to talk about trading

and our ideas, and sometimes we just meet at our houses and barbeque together while talking about trading. It's fun!" – Markus Heitkoetter

*This real life story is adapted from TRADERS' magazine, December 2013. (Source: www.tradersonline-mag.com)

Chapter 19: Important Questions Traders Should Ask Themselves

CHF JPY

"Only execute the trade when the chart matches your plan, if it doesn't – no trade." – Gavin Knoesen

Intelligent speculation includes some salient aspects like opening of trades, trade management, emotions control and strategy optimization. There is no way around the fact that these salient aspects can never be avoided by active traders, but our attitudes towards them can make a big difference between good and bad trading habits. These are the questions traders need to ask themselves often and often:

Did I open my trade according to my entry criteria?

It's imperative that you open a trade according to strict entry criteria. Trading discipline entails your refusal to trade a setup that doesn't match your entry criteria; no matter how attractive the setup is. Trades shouldn't be opened randomly. No matter what the news shows or how attractive the markets are, we won't open any trades until our setups appear. You make mistakes only when you don't follow your trading rules. A loss trade isn't a mistake, provided that you opened the trade according to your entry rules. A trade that's opened in violation of your entry rules is a mistake – whether it results in profits or loss.

Did I follow my trade management plan when the trade was open? If not, why?

This is one of the reasons why many traders find trading difficult: they're unable to stick to their trading plans after they enter the market. A swing trader opens a trade and quickly closes it after about a 10-pip gain, for the fear of a price reversal. An intraday trader decides to run a negative position for several more days with the hope that the price could turn in their favour. These attitudes are bad. You need to know that once you enter the market – irrespective of how great your signal is – trading becomes managerial. It's your trade management and exit techniques that will ultimately determine your long-term success, and this has nothing to do with your trading accuracy. When you have open positions, never forget to stick to your breakeven rule (if any), trailing stop rule (if any), trading duration rule and exit rules. Anyone who constantly violates their trading management rules needs psychological help.

What was my reaction after the trade was closed?

If you traded flawlessly, the outcome didn't matter. Sane traders gauge their success by how flawlessly they execute their trades, not by how much they make or lose. If the AUDJPY moves significantly in your favour, it makes little difference to how you feel when it moves significantly against you. A significant movement in the market is a significant movement. If the AUDJPY moves significantly against you, it makes little difference than when it moves significantly in your favour. An adverse movement has negligible effect on good risk managers; whereas a favourable movement has satisfactory effect on their portfolios. Traders occasionally sustain negativity but they don't want to take responsibility for that, they think they've been treated unfairly when the markets simply move without having anyone in mind. We must take responsibility when we make a profit and when we make a loss.

Is there any way I can optimize my trading strategy?

Permanently victorious traders use conservative trading methods for long-term objectives. It doesn't matter whether the methods are boring or not. Anyone looking for thrill may try sky-diving or bungee jumping. The real trading breakthrough has to do with finding a good setup rule and trading it constantly. A negative expectancy system needs improvement, but a positive expectancy system doesn't need that. This doesn't mean that the positive expectancy system can't have losing streaks. During a losing streak which may be normally protracted, it's sad that an average trade abandons a good system when it's on the brink of a winning streak. The newly found system can either start losing or winning right away; only to later begin to experience an opposite streak. You oughtn't to be discouraged even if your strategy is no longer interesting. Stick to it as long as it helps you make money. And don't forget that it's possible to keep your account safe no matter what the market does.

Conclusion

It's imperative that you stick to your winning strategy – even if it's no longer interesting. Your trading strategy may not be interesting, but keep on using it as long as it helps you obtain average winners that are bigger than average losers over a long period of time.

"Many people hold trading in the same regard as gambling but it is an unfair comparison. Trading is not gambling unless you are trading blindly, randomly, without adhering to a trading plan and completely ignoring any risk management." – Stuart McPhee

Chapter 20: When Fundamental Analysis Fails

GBP NZD

"Everyone is following the economy, but I'm following the market." – Joe Granville

There are those who invest successfully using only fundamental figures and there those who successfully trade using only technical analysis. There are those who combine the two types of analyses and make money.

Nevertheless, I can see that many investors believe so much in fundamental analysis that they refuse to smooth their orders when caught on the wrong side of the market direction, because the fundamentals support the wrong side. I'm not saying that fundamental analysis doesn't work; it works, but it isn't a Golden Goose trading method, for there are investors/traders who lose heavily despite the fact that they position their orders according to the fundamentals that are affecting the instruments they're interested in.

When fundamental analysis fails, what do you do? What you can do to survive and become victorious requires that you look beyond fundamental analysis. Further chapters will shed more light on this.

No type of analysis is perfect: therefore it's risk control that can make one survive the vagaries of the markets. Fundamentals or no fundamentals, you need to know what really works in the market. Joe Granville of blessed memory is quoted as saying that he followed the market when everybody followed the economy. Joe, who focused on the market, was a highly respected and successful trading expert.

One profitable itinerant speculator once declared that the only thing that we need in order to make money in the market is to understand how the market works. That's a fact. Most veteran traders acknowledge this fact. The knowledge of how the market works is what would make you a profitable trader.

For example, there are a few stages of investors' attitudes in a bear market. Investors may be overconfident and greedy, thinking that the price is too cheap and could turn in their favour anytime. At this time, most bears are ecstatic about pushing the price further south, but investors would keep on buying. Then there would be a stage of lack of dread and conservation, which causes investors to become sober and cautious because the market keeps on plunging. The falling price makes some investors angry and shameful. Then there would be another stage of total apathy and frustration when the market has become extremely oversold and it's really ready to shift gears and start a new long-term bullish bias, that's when investors would lose confidence in the market and stay out altogether (or leave their positions for the worst that could happen). The timing of the masses would continue to be wrong.

Many traders are making money in the markets in spite of economic problems in developed countries. Sometimes, it's not uncommon to see the market going up when negative data is being released. Sometimes, you'll see a market plunging despite good figures that are being published. It just depends, if a bad figure that's just been released is the most encouraging among similar figures released in the past several months or years, it might have a positive impact on the market rather than a negative one.

This chapter ends with the quote below:

"Most traders fail because they think they know more than the markets… I say humility because to me every time I caught myself saying 'oh this market has to be a buy because it can't go any lower' really is a statement of ego, which is another way of pretending you know more than the market." – John Person

Chapter 21: The Risk-to-Reward of 1 to 2 – a Magic Ratio

EUR AUD

The Ideal Positive Expectancy

"It is especially in short-term trading, with a wealth of trading signals, that consistent trading in the overall trend direction pays off." – Arne and Falk Elsner

One of the big factors in trading success is to think in terms of the risk-to-reward ratio (RRR). That's your risk in terms of the potential reward. You know, for you to survive in the markets, you have to target at least two dollars for every dollar you risk.

Some target three, four, five or more dollars for each dollar they risk; which is fine. This is the logic behind positive expectancy. In contrast to this, anyone who risks two, three, five… two hundred or five hundred dollars to target one dollar or a few dollars is using a negative expectancy approach. Anyone who doesn't use stops and who's determined to run the losses till they break even is using a negative (worse) expectancy approach. The fact is: anyone using a negative expectancy approach can't last long in the markets.

The Benefits of the RRR of 1:2

Now, let's go back to the idea of 1:2. In all the years of my grappling with the markets, I've seen that the RRR of 1:2 is the most optimal one. These are some of the reasons.

1. The 1:2 expectancy is the least that should be sought by sensible traders. Risking one dollar to target less than two dollars is really not in the trader's best interest.

2. With optimal stops and targets, the ratio 1:2 is more easily achieved than 1:3, 1:4, 1:5… 1:10 etc. While a higher RRR like 1:5 requires a hit rate of 20% or less to attain profits, it's very difficult to practice, requires a high level of discipline and requires an unending patience to run the winners. How many traders can surmount the emotional hurdles?

3. With rational and logical fine-tuning of one's strategy, one might be able to achieve a hit rate of 40% or more over time, thus the RRR of 1:2 is enough to make one a consistent winner.

4. The best trending pairs and crosses in Forex are often the ones most analysts tend to ignore. Remember that you need price movement before you can make money. No movement in the price, no profits/loss. If you trade highly trending Forex instruments, it's more probable that you will achieve good results with the expectancy of 1:2 so that your stops/targets are triggered quickly as you look at short-term and medium-term biases. When more liquid and highly trending trading instruments are sought and played, the possibility of roll-downs is reduced while the rise in equity becomes noticeable. When the EURAUD is bullish, you need not give yourself any headache by going for complicated analysis. When the cross is bullish, you will see the price going upwards.

5. If you use the RRR of 1:2, it will be possible for you to reach breakeven with a hit rate of 33.3%. This means that recent losses are easily recovered. The risk-to-reward of 1:2 is indeed a magic ratio!

Conclusion

It's very crucial that we acknowledge that we can't be correct most of the time, or often more than half of all our orders. Our hit rate may be far lower than that, but we'll become profitable if we know how to handle our negative and positive trades, things over which we have control (especially when it comes to their effect on our portfolio over time). Using high lot sizes relative to our portfolio size is like courting financial disaster. It's thus far safer to stake a maximum of 1% per trade while targeting at least two dollars for each dollar that is at stake.

This chapter ends with the quote below:

"It takes patience and a strong commitment to study the markets and identify good setups... But in the end, it's worth it. If you carefully select high probability setups, you'll trade more profitably and you'll be more satisfied with your performance." – Joe Ross

Chapter 22: What Would Happen Next to the EURUSD?

CHF USD

"It is not so important to be right, but how to make money when you are right." – Ivan Hoff

I remember what happened at one interesting trading conference I attended about five months ago. It was an interesting conference indeed. At one stage, the moderator showed us a EURUSD chart (whose dominant trend was bullish, but the short-term trend was bearish) and asked us this question:

Where do you think the price will go next?

There was silence in the hall. Predicting the future is a great challenge; plus it's senseless to talk about the future price action with an utmost certainty. A few traders stood up and tried to give their opinions. I later stood up, took the microphone and said that two things could happen at that juncture: the price could turn in favour of the dominant trend which would continue OR the short-term bearish correction could actually be the beginning of a strong bearish outlook. Was I wrong?

One man quickly got up to announce that I was wrong. He said that the price MUST turn upwards since the dominant trend was bullish. I kept quiet. Can you see how traders showcase the mindset that can endanger their career?

This was a bone of contention; some seriously thought the pullback would end up blending with the overall trend. But the reality was that it could be the beginning of another long term reverse trend.

Being opinionated is a not a good thing in trading. Those who have enjoyed lasting success in the markets know how to admit their errors, get out of losing trades and look for the next signals which may be profitable. However, opinionated traders never admit their mistakes and often take the decision to run their loss for as long as the market goes contrary to them. An opinionated trader may even be confident enough to open a very large position (like 20% or 40% risk), believing that the price MUST go in their favour. The person may even refuse to put a stop for disaster prevention

Was the man right? Yes, he was right, but the short-term correction took the price downwards by up to 500 pips before the price went in the direction of the dominant bias. In some cases, the market could even go down by over 1,500 pips within the next few weeks before any meaningful reversal, if that would happen at all. Can you see how people make decisions that have adverse effects on their portfolios?

Was I also right? Yes. I gave two possibilities of the price direction – either up or down. In order to benefit from this expectation or ensure that an adverse movement doesn't affect my portfolio, I truncate my loss when I'm wrong and give my gain some leeway when I'm right. I'm not opinionated: I know what to do whenever I'm proven right or wrong.

Being Bearish or Bullish Makes No Difference

It's common for many a trader to say "I'm bearish/bullish on this market." That doesn't make any difference. What would happen when a swing trader goes short in a market because they hears a scalper announcing being bearish? When a position trader says they is bullish, do you think an intraday trader can make a 'fool-proof' long trade?

I look at a EURUSD chart and I say I'm bearish, but you look at it and say you're bullish. A chart is a chart, plus both the bear and the bull can make money in the same market. When a dominantly bearish market rallies by over 600 pips, the bull can make some gains. In the same market, the bear can also make some gain when the price pulls back in the direction of the dominant bias in which the buying or selling is prevalent – what makes the difference are the timing methods and trading styles.

Being bullish or bearish makes no difference. What makes a difference is your respect for the realities taking place in the markets. A confirmation of a reversal wouldn't happen overnight; it takes days or sometimes, weeks. The transition from a downtrend to an uptrend doesn't happen in a flash; instead there would be a gradual thinning out of the downtrend which then translates into an uptrend, causing lower highs amidst consolidation and swing lows. No matter how significant a counter-trend bullish or bearish engulfing candle pattern is, it doesn't mean the trend is over, unless the next series of candles continue to hold onto the reversal long enough. Otherwise, the significant bearish or bullish engulfing pattern may be a spike which gives traders an excellent opportunity to enter the market on a good bargain.

Conclusion

The FX markets are among the most liquid trading markets in the world, and therefore, when a strongly trending instrument assumes an established bias, it may go on longer than anticipated. In the face of this fact, a reversal in the context of the established bias may either be transitory or be a start of a protracted movement in the opposite direction. Rather than being opinionated about a direction, you'll help yourself by aborting your losers and riding your winners – the only way to face the vagaries of the markets victoriously.

This fact is summed up in the quote below:

"I spend my day trying to make myself as happy and relaxed as I can be. If I have positions going against me, I get right out. If they are going for me, I keep them." – Paul Tudor Jones

Chapter 23: I Can't Win Trading Competitions

CADGBP

"We've seen plenty of traders over the years make huge returns on their accounts, well over 1,000 per cent in a relatively short period of time, but as soon as they hit a drawdown period they just as quickly give it all back. This is because they were trading well beyond risk limits in the first place." – **Charlie Burton**

The currency markets have many benefits that are no longer secrets: the biggest daily turnover, the inability of Smart Money to control the markets permanently to their favour, interesting fundamentals, high liquidity, 24-hour availability, low spreads, etc. As a result of the increasing popularity of the markets, many types of programs are coming up in the financial industry; and one of them is trading competitions.

I once participated in some of the competitions and never won a single one. In spite of my trading knowledge, I've never even ended in the top 50, not to mention the second or third position. Why?

On demo and live accounts, I don't usually risk more than 0.5% or at most 1% per trade. I need to do this consistently so that it becomes my second nature. Trading is a game of survival, but in those kinds of competitions, even if I make 2,000 pips in a month, my profits would only be 10% or 20%. Now, someone else could make less than 500 pips in a month and achieve 500% profits. The difference lies in the amount of risk per trade. Can you now see why I can't win a trading contest?

In most competitions, a contestant who achieves the highest returns within the shortest time duration is usually declared the winner. A trading competition – usually a demo accounts competition – tends to last for one week or one month only. Every competitor thus strives to achieve hundreds or thousands of percent of returns during the short period. I've seen a competition in which a participant made 3,000% returns in less than one week! I've seen a trading competition in which a participant made 700% returns in a month. Does this means they're the most proficient traders on the planet? The answer is NO.

When the market is favourable to your trading method, you'll be making money with new orders, no matter what. A winning streak can last for days, weeks or months, before it's alternated by a losing streak (before another winning streak comes again). It's too common that most people who make money in winning streaks give back more than their profits during losing streaks, as a result of excessively high stakes and lack of risk control methods.

Most types of trading competitions encourage people to make the highest possible money as quickly as possible. This kind of indoctrination can't favour traders that aspire to a lasting career. Just as speculators who get hundreds of percent of profits because of excessively big position sizes, but soon they're no longer in the markets; one who risks too much per trade is a gambler, but one who takes risk control methods seriously is a real trader. When a competing gambler is in a winning streak, they can make hundreds or thousands of percentage returns when 20%, 30%, 40%, 50% or 60% (or more) of the portfolio is risked per trade. Nevertheless, the higher the stake per trade, the higher the loss or the drawdown when something goes contrary to the trading method. That's why some of the so-called expert traders or trading champions later crashed and burned in the markets. They will still tell you trading is great and they can trade very well, but they're no longer in the markets because their suicide trading methods backfired at them.

Would you prefer to get rich quickly and have a temporary career or would you want to make small and constant gains? What matters most to you: the safety of your account or big profits as soon as possible?

There are also certain trading competitions in which organizers rule that winners must accurately predict the exact price of a particular trading instrument within a specific period. Isn't that hard? Market wizards all agree that future prices can't be predicted, yet we can harness gains from them. How can I predict the exact future prices when I'm not clairvoyant or psychic? If psychics could even do that, I guess they'd have become billionaire traders. Should you predict an exact future price within a specific period and win, it is by pure chance.

The Types of Trading Competitions I Can Win

There are types of trading competitions I can win, but sadly, they're not that common in the Forex world.

I can win a trading competition that rules that winners would be those whose accounts are still intact and positive after making 1,000 trades (or at least 500 trades) within some years. How many gamblers can win that type of competition? I can win a competition that gives awards to those who achieve the least amount of drawdowns after several months or years. I can win a trading competition that recognizes contestants who makes most pips, not most profits within several months.

Yes, if that kind of trading competition allows contestants to compete for ten months or even years, I can win it. One week or one month is definitely too short to test the reliability of a trading system.

A good trader is someone who deals with losing streaks successfully and recovers from them, not someone who makes great profits in winning streaks and crashes in losing streaks.

The most important thing a good trader can do is to keep an account permanently safe in the face of the vagaries of the markets.

Making profits is a secondary aim, for there must be an intact capital before profits can be made. If the capital is gone, there's no means of carrying out additional transactions that could be successful. One best way of keeping our accounts safe is to learn how permanently victorious traders have managed to keep their portfolios safe for decades.

Conclusion

Most speculators who've made billions of dollars from the markets have become extremely rich because their portfolios are huge and they make relatively small, consistent gains. They haven't become billionaires because they achieved 100% gains over and over and over again within very short time periods. They achieve their aims by looking for low risk investment opportunities and capitalizing on them by giving their winners enough leeway. This is easier said than done, for most traders find it difficult to run their winners – it really is difficult. But it's essential for long-term survival.

This chapter ends with the quote below:

"Pace yourself, take small gains and small losses, trading is not a sprint towards riches, it's a marathon towards financial independency." – Alpesh Patel

Chapter 24: The Most Important Goal in Trading

JPY EUR

"Being profitable in the long run with trading, and all investing for that matter, is about cutting losses and letting profits run. Although it's a hearsay thing of ages, statistical expectancy actually proofs the saying mathematical. It's not about being right or wrong but handling both profits and losses well." – **Dirk Vandycke**

Whether you're a beginner trader or an experienced trader, you need to know that the most important goal in trading is the permanent safety of your capital. When the fund in your account is gone, what can you use to make additional transactions? You'll need to replenish the account or open another one. But when the fund in your account is intact – no matter the vagaries of the markets – there'll come some periods when you'll make profits. Profits come on existing accounts, not defunct accounts.

Sadly, too many people are so obsessed with making money that they forget or neglect the principles that can keep their account safe. One great piece of advice is attributed to the Oracle of Omaha, Warren Buffett. He said that there are two trading rules:

1. Don't lose your money!

2. Never forget rule one!

Honestly, there's nothing more important in trading than the rules above. All other rules are secondary.

You may not want to agree with me over this. Many people may be making noises in forums and other social community places for traders, saying that there are other things that are more important than the fact above. But bear it in mind that anybody can say anything about the market and you don't need to be a guru, or have a fancy university degree, or show your muscle or be a rational person before you can voice your opinions about the markets. All you need is to have a big mouth and you'll get more and more followers. In reality, most of the 'big mouths' are being forced shut when the market shows them its true colour.

The vagaries of the markets aren't a curse, but they're rather a blessing that enables us to make gains in the markets. The only thing the market can do is to move sideways, up or down. This truth will ever remain timeless and therefore, those who know how to anticipate the moves will be victorious.

No matter what your aims and ambitions are as a trader, the most important thing you can bear in mind is the safety of your portfolio. This goal is not difficult to achieve, provided you know how to go about it. Some of our future chapters will explain how the goal can be realised.

"Most people find Forex trading very attractive because it gives a person complete control, breaking free of all the rules from their day to day life. Unfortunately the Forex market requires rules, structure and consistency at an even more intense level than your daily life does. So if you're looking to operate 'rule free', then trading is probably not for you." – Graham Blackmore (Source: Trade2win.com)

Chapter 25: Are Top Athletes Richer than Top Fund Managers?

NZD CAD

"If you understand this way of thinking – that by taking smart risks you can make money over time – it will improve your willingness to take risks." **Bruce Bower**

What is the answer to the question that forms the topic of this chapter? The answer is a big NO!

Floyd Mayweather, LeBron James, Cristiano Ronaldo, Tiger Woods, Roger Federer, Lewis Hamilton, Mahendra Singh Dhoni, Cliff Lee, Usain Bolt, etc. Each of these stars is one of the best in their respective fields, and no doubt, they've achieved success and fame that billions of people can only dream of. Yet, each of them is still poor when compared to the highest paid fund managers in the world.

If you want to know what each of the star athletes mentioned here earns, you will need to do the research yourself. On Buzz.money.cnn.com, Jesse Solomon shows a list of the ten highest paid hedge fund managers in 2013: David Tepper, Steven Cohen, John Paulson, James Simons, Kenneth Griffin, Israel Englander, Leon Cooperman, Lawrence Robbins, Dan Loebb and Paul Tudor Jones.

David Tepper earned $3.5 billion last year. In 2009, he earned some $4 billion. He's currently worth $10 billion. David's riches are even far more surpassed by those of some market legends like Carl Icahn ($24.5 billion) and George Soros ($26.5 billion). I don't even want to mention the Wizard/Sage/Oracle of Omaha.

How much do you think a boxing champion like Floyd Mayweather earned? He earned $105 million, thus currently making him the highest paid athlete in the world. Nevertheless, the tenth highest paid hedge fund manager is Paul Tudor Jones who got a pay check of $600 million in 2013. This means that Paul is more than five times richer than Floyd in terms of income last year. Paul's net worth is $4.5 billion.

The highest paid soccer player in the world at the time of writing is Cristiano Ronaldo, with less than $100 million in total earnings per annum; yet his income is more than six times smaller than that of the tenth highest paid fund manager in the world.

Do you now see my point? The world of trading has produced many billionaires – past and present. These traders are extremely rich and the incomes of the star athletes pale into insignificance when compared to the earnings of those fund managers.

It's true that top athletes enjoy the heavy glare of publicity and are far more popular because of myriads of fans the world over. Some professional traders aren't famous because they trade behind their computers in the comfort of their offices. Most people don't know them, save interested individuals who are mostly traders/investors themselves. When many football fans talk about how rich their favourite players are, they are often not aware that some professional traders are far richer than them.

With a worth of $1.1 billion, the New York Knicks are the most valuable team in NBA for 2013 (with revenue of $243 million for that year). Real Madrid is the most valuable sports team, worth $3.3 billion (with revenue of roughly $700 million per annum). However, David Tepper, who is not the richest trader in the world (only the highest paid for the year 2013) is far richer than the New York Knicks and Real Madrid combined. According to Jesse, the top 25 fund managers took home $21 billion among themselves last year.

You should congratulate yourself on being a trader, irrespective of your experiences in the markets. The richest traders didn't become rich overnight, nor did the richest athletes, for most of them had very humble beginnings. By adjusting your trading approaches to achieve everlasting triumph and by sticking to those approaches, you'll soon reach financial freedom (though you may not attain the list of the highest paid traders).

Another quote from Bruce Bower ends this chapter:

"Focus on making good risk/reward decisions, keeping losses small, and you will start to become profitable."

Chapter 26: Why We Want You to Become a Successful Trader

AUDCAD

A Step Between Penury and Solvency

"Once you take the desire to make money out of your trading and put in the desire to do what good traders do, your mindset shifts and allows you to make more good decisions." – Craig Cobb

Alan (names in this chapter have been changed) has reached the end of his tether. His handiwork is not enough to feed him with staple foods, not to mention paying his rent. He's getting old and he needs to get married so that he can start a family, but he can't even afford the lowest-key wedding ceremony. He wants to gather some money for his wedding. He applies to a chemical factory and he's hired immediately. It happens that anyone who applies there will be hired immediately because no educational background is required. Besides, the strongest man in the world can't work in the factory for one year.

Alan discovers that the working conditions are so ignominiously abject. Apart from the fact that you must work for a minimum of 12 hours per day (84 hours per week), with very hard labour, factory safety has a zero rating and the pungent chemical itself carries a major health hazard. If you get injured, you'll be fired with no first aid. The monthly salary is less than $100. You are penalized for coming late to work and $3 is deducted from your salary per day if you're absent, even if your absence is due to heath issues.

Alan likes to work hard and he's hardy, yet he quits the job in less than three weeks. The stinking chemical is taking tolls on his health.

Samson's wife is dead, leaving three children for him to take care of. Samson believes the only way to honour the memory of his dearly beloved wife is to take good care of her children. Although his income is not that much, he manages the money well so that the children can attend school and have access to a basic balanced diet.

Suddenly, Samson's boss announces that the firm is no longer making profits and all the employees will be laid off in a month's time. The firm folds up. Since then, Samson has been looking for a job – any job – without success. He lives in a country where over 40% of able-bodied citizens are unemployed. The kids are now suffering: they're out of school and malnourished.

Alisa is a full-time housewife and a responsible mom. She's resigned from her work in order to attend to her kids, for she's worried that her kids may suffer some disadvantages if she and her hubby have to stay away from home for economic reasons.

Alisa, however, perceives that her husband's income would be barely enough to sustain the family. Therefore, she needs to look for some passive income to supplement the family's income and possibly safeguard their future.

Life is full of risk. Someone loses an election after a huge amount of money has been spent. That doesn't make it improper to spend money on elections. Someone starts a transportation business and ends up running at a loss. That doesn't mean that transportation business is bad. Someone loses his child after spending a fortune to bring them up and educate them. That doesn't mean it's wasteful to take care of one's children. Someone purchases some valuables that are eventually stolen, but that doesn't mean it's wrong to buy valuables. A movie or an album is produced, but it does not sell well (a floundering title or a crashing failure). Do we then need to tell people to abstain from movie or album production? A dear brother is ill and hospitalized. We pray fervently for his recovery; yet he dies. Does that mean prayers are useless? Someone's house is destroyed in a natural disaster, but it doesn't mean we should be preaching against owning a home. Someone's marriage crashes after spending huge sums on the union. Does that mean it's wrong to get married? Someone has an accident with his car. Does that mean one shouldn't buy a car? The list could go on. Doctors jailed. Ferries capsize. Mines explode, etc. The list of professional hazards out of trading is inexhaustible.

The fact that some people lose in trading doesn't make it a bad career. This is in a huge contrast to what members of the public believe. If they see one negative trade, they start preaching to people to avoid trading like a plague. These are the people that suffer losses in other areas of life but they don't see bad things in them. If you don't know successful traders, there are many of them.

Many people see trading as being risky. Yet, they lose heavily in other aspects of life. The majority of people start small scale businesses; but statistics shows that over 90% of small scale businesses fail within their first three years. Think of an easy job, millions of people are also thinking of doing that job. The economy is already glutted. Generally, the jobs and trades that every Tom, Dick and Harry finds easy to do or start scarcely bring financial freedom. The kinds of jobs that bring real financial freedom – like trading the markets – are what most people abhor and find extremely challenging.

Some educated people are suffering because they believe in 'I beg to apply' mentality. After all, that's the reason why most people go to college. One of the most difficult things one can do now is to seek and get a good job. The number of school leavers continues to outpace the number of jobs created and the situation has high chances of getting worse.

I know somebody who wanted to get employed in a popular oil company. He was told to get a master's degree, for he had only a bachelor's degree then. He enrolled in a master's degree program. After he completed the program, he went back to the oil company, only to be told that there was no vacancy for him. While his degrees aren't a disadvantage to him, must he work for an oil company? Can you ask Deron Wagner or Anton Kreil to go for master's degrees before you employ them?

Without financial freedom, the future looks bleak indeed. Most private companies don't have retirement plans for their employees, even in developed lands. Most companies and organizations now prefer contract staff. Do you want to put your financial destiny in the hands of your boss?

You may be working right now (or even self-employed), but do you think people will still need your services at old age? If you're a plumber or a driver, would people still give you jobs to do at old age, when there are numerous young men who are also competent? Have you even saved enough money for your old age, or do you expect your children to support you then?

Growing older is no offence: it's a privilege. Nevertheless, some employers wouldn't consider you if you're above a certain young age. They'll tell you: "Applicants who are above the age of 25 need not apply." Can they ever say that to David Tepper or David Harding?

Nothing ventured, nothing gained; and to do nothing is to become nothing. If you can become a successful trader, you'll attain financial freedom. You aren't going to be retired, for you'll continue to trade in your old age. You'll trade leisurely and effortlessly and get rewarded. People like Van K. Tharp and Joe Ross are elderly traders and they're successful.

The older you become and the more years of experience you gain, the more valuable and the more sought-after you'll become.

Trading is a serious business. We want you to become a successful trader. While people complain of economic hardships, you'll only be smiling all the way to your bank.

This chapter ends with the quote below:

"…Trading is the art of paying the price for something you want. It is the art of regarding fear as the greatest sin, and giving up as the greatest mistake. It is the art of accepting failure as a step toward victory." – Roy Longstreet

Chapter 27: The Easiest Ways to Turn Losses into Profits

CADUSD

"Isn't the promised reward of greater independence, financial freedom, and life choices worth the risk?" –
Louise Bedford

Anyone who says trading is easy is telling a lie. Anyone who says success in trading isn't possible is also telling a lie. Trading is challenging as well as rewarding. The challenges are the blessings that awaken the trading genius in us.

Celebrated psychics have made both accurate and failed predictions. If I was sure I could predict the future with the utmost certainty, I'd rather buy lotto tickets and enter my lucky numbers. Before the results were announced, I'd start smiling on the way to my bank because I knew I couldn't lose! By behaving as though we know what the market will do, we tend to think we're very smart, but the market is kind enough to remind us occasionally that we're not always smart. If you remember that you're a student of the market, that will be your saving grace.

Most people find trading difficult, due to some preconceived notions. Trading is emotional, for the results of our decisions are seen on our portfolios immediately. Because of certain preconceived notions, inexperienced and undisciplined traders inadvertently maximize their negativity and minimize their positivity: experienced and disciplined traders do exactly otherwise.

Turning Losing Approaches
Into Winning Approaches

How can you turn losses into profits? Your past trading records can't be changed but your future trading records can be satisfactory if you determine to stop using trading approaches that bring you frequent losses over a long period of time.

The market has symmetry: if you do something and make money, you would have lost if you had done the opposite. For example, when you sold the AUDJPY and lost 200 pips, that means you could have made a profit of 200 pips if you had bought it. Therefore you need to stop doing what brings you losses and try to do it the other way round. Here are a few examples:

1. One secret in trading is that less popular trading instruments are more easily predicted than the popular ones. The less popular pairs have very little noise affecting them and tend to move in more predictable manners. The EURAUD is thus more easily predictable than the EURUSD, since the EURUSD is very popular and therefore much affected by noise. It's the noise that causes a lot of false signals on the pair. The CHFJPY is more easily predicted than the USDJPY. If you're using a trend-following approach, you'll find that it works far better on less popular currency trading instruments. Counter-trend methods tend to work better on popular pairs; and vice versa on less popular pairs.

2. If you discover that you're more prone to making more money on some pair(s) than the other(s), you need to concentrate on the pair(s) that favour your trading system most.

3. When you discover that you tend to make more money on Forex markets than futures markets, you may want to give Forex markets some serious thought.

4. People who lose money by setting risk that's much bigger than reward would surely do themselves a big favour by reversing that: they will need to set reward that's greater than risk. That means better RRR (like 1:2, 1:3 or more).

5. If failure to use (optimal) stops constantly has adverse effects on your portfolio, please try to start using (optimal) stops from now on. The stop is not a perfect money management tool – no money management tool is perfect – but the eventual benefit outweighs the short-term disadvantage. That's your life insurance in the markets.

6. If you lose money by cutting your winners and running your losers, you'll start making money when you cut your losers and run your winners.

7. If you make more money on Monday with, say, swing trading, then you'll want to continue doing that. Those who lose on Fridays may want to stop trading on Fridays. If you discover that your hit rate increases on Tuesdays, Wednesdays and Thursdays, you may want to take trading seriously on those days. If you observe that you make money the most in London sessions, you may want to stop trading the Tokyo session; and the other way round.

8. If you often lose when you pick tops and bottoms, then you may want to consider selling at bottoms and buying at tops. If you have a strategy that loses too much (always) for long periods of time; if that strategy loses more money in protracted losing streaks than it makes in short-term winning streaks, then you'll experience your breakthrough if you open opposite orders when the strategy gives you signals, for example going short when it gives a 'buy' signal.

Is a higher hit rate part of the solution? A gambler that uses a system with 90% hit rate can still ruin their portfolio; whereas a skilled risk manager can have a permanently satisfactory and rewarding career with only 40% hit rate. With some effort, the hit rate can be improved or some losing trades can be avoided by applying filters and/or staying out of a losing streak. Indeed, one way of improving our trading results is to try to avoid some bogus signals as well. We have some ways of doing this, but that will be the subject of another chapter.

Conclusion

In summary, the easiest way to turn consistent losing into consistent profiting is to change your trading approaches according to principles that ensure success in the markets. Stop doing what doesn't work for you and embrace what works for you. If something makes you lose constantly, you'll make money by going contrary to it.

This chapter concludes with the quote below:

"By matching the amount of risk you take with your tolerance for risk, you can trade more calmly, and that usually means you'll trade more profitably." – Joe Ross

Chapter 28: The Most Important Factor Behind Traders' Failure – Part 1

JPY GBP

"No methodology will work unless you are able to develop the proper mindset to follow it." – **Dave Landry**

The world of trading is full of things that work and things that don't work. To be honest, there are many successful traders who are also teaching people how to become successful. There are many signals providers who provide winning signals. There are many strategies that work and there are many programs, like webinars and trading rooms, which can help other traders to improve significantly. Unfortunately, in spite of these, the percentage of losers still remains above 90%. Why?

There is a primary reason for that (other reasons are merely secondary). The human mind isn't wired to trade properly – unless the mind is trained to adapt to the seemingly 'strange' but helpful approaches that guarantee one's survival. We don't find it easy to do the things that can ensure our permanent triumph. What we find easy to do are things that agree with our faulty mindset, but which can't help us in the long run. If you can't ride your winners, it's because your mindset is against that, and you'll always find it difficult to do. Even if a swing trading system has a high hit rate, it won't make money if profits aren't allowed to run.

For instance, most motorists obey traffic rules because they want to avoid the legal consequences for not doing so, not because they take their own safety seriously. Why should the use of a helmet be enforced for bikers? Don't they know that the use of a helmet is for their own safety? They know, but they still find it easier not to put on the helmet than to put on one. That's the human mindset.

It's known that making or receiving phone calls while driving is dangerous (for the brain of a driver who does that doesn't operate any better than the brain of a drunkard), yet some drivers still do it.

I once took a taxi. While the driver was driving me, his phone began to ring over and over again. He sensed that the call was very important, so he located a suitable place to park, stopped and took the call. After that, he continued the journey. What the man did might look stupid in the eyes of most drivers. How could he begin to look for a place to park simply because he wanted to receive a mere call? In contrast, most drivers would prefer to answer the call while driving – the thought of tickets being the only thing that can prevent them from doing that.

In the world of retail trading where retail traders are allowed to trade as they like, it's no wonder that they often end up losing. Even if they know what they can do to safeguard their accounts in the face of the vagaries of the markets, they are prone to ignore that because of irrational emotions. If retail traders could be forced and micromanaged to do the right things while trading, the percentage of losers would decrease dramatically, but such a thing isn't possible.

For example, false breakouts are common in consolidating market phases, and trading them would have adverse effects on our portfolios if we are invested for the long-term. You may have sworn never to trade a consolidating market, but because of the faulty mindset, you suddenly open a position in a consolidating market because you feel the position is promising. You have sworn to respect your stops, but you suddenly see yourself running a gargantuan negative position. Obviously, you have refused to smooth the position because you feel it may go back to the entry price.

When institutional traders cover their positions, the market pulls back, but the noobs think they can follow the direction of the pullback. When you see a significant bias that occurs without plausible economic reasons, the bias can be transitory and the pullback might even be a new protracted market outlook. You have sworn to be a swing trader or position trader, opening a few trades per month or week, but you suddenly start scalping or opening too many positions that you close within 24 hours because of too much negativity. You call yourself a position trader or an investor, but you suddenly find yourself watching the one-minute chart because you can't sleep while you have open positions. You know, a position trader has got nothing to do with one-minute charts. You think new significant biases may start and you want to be an early bird by looking at one-minute charts.

You are a swing/position trader and thus you need to use wide stops so that you can create more room for normal market fluctuations. But you find yourself using stops that are too tight: you don't want to allow a trade to move against you by a few or several pips and you call yourself a position trader! Tight stops cause frequent losses – even trades that ought to end up winning would be stopped out if the stops are too tight.

Doing the right thing require discipline, even if it makes you look stupid sometimes. You've got to find a way to condition your mind to do the right things, no matter what. That's what pays in the long run. It's better to look for ways to control losing streaks than to look for 'wise' trading rules that don't improve any statistics. This is what will ultimately help you by making you avoid severe roll-downs. It's after you survive severe roll-downs that you can hope to make some gains.

This chapter ends with the quote below:

"One thing is sure: a trading strategy that is not adapted to the traders individual preferences concerning philosophy, trading frequency or time exposure will not generate profits simply because it will not be followed." – David Pieper

Chapter 29: The Most Important Factor Behind Traders' Failure – Part 2

NZD AUD

"Our mind is our enemy." – Tom Hougaard

Our mind is really our foe, especially when we find it extremely difficult to do what is in our best interest. Doing the right things tends to make us uncomfortable initially, unless we train our mind to adapt to doing the right things until it becomes our second nature. In the previous chapter, I mentioned how drivers and motorcyclists need to be forced to do what is in their best interest and the best interest of their loved ones (as well as that of members of the public).

It's well known that smokers are liable to die young. A few years ago, I visited an elderly man who is the father of one of my friends. He was glad to see me. After some time, he reached for his drawer and took out a cigarette. He lit it and started smoking. The elderly man noticed that I wasn't happy that he was smoking. I was concerned about his health, for he looked a bit emaciated. Before I could speak, he said:

"Young man, I know you aren't happy that I'm smoking, but that's not your business. I've been smoking since before you and my son were born. I know cigars are dangerous to my health, but mind you, if my health deteriorates and I die, it's nobody's business. Nicotine is thought to be poisonous; yet I buy it with my money and take it into my body. It's my body and my life, not your body or my son's body. If what I do can affect my life, it's nobody's business. It's my life and it's not your concern if I lose it. I'll smoke till I die. Whether I smoke or not, it's something that'll cause my death. Your friend has accepted this fact and has stopped remonstrating with me. I've told my children that if I die today, I should be buried quickly so that I don't cause a stench in the neighbourhood."

What does this have to do with trading? Many traders who know the things that won't pay them in the markets still find those things irresistible. This is the most important reason why most traders won't make it. Below, you can read four things that will guarantee your failure in the markets. If you avoid those things, your success is then guaranteed.

Four Things that will Guarantee your Failure in the Markets

1. *Thinking that risk control isn't very crucial.* Risk control is one of the major factors that contribute to your everlasting success in the market. If you don't know what it is, you'd better learn it and start applying it. If you know it already, you'd better start applying it with strict religiosity.

2. *Thinking that you know everything.* It's unfortunate that many traders feel that they know what a price is going to do next. We tend to feel we're hot, but the markets sometimes remind us that we're cold. The expert traders' saving grace is that they never forget they're students of the markets. It's thus helpful to trade what you see and properly manage your trades. It's by far more helpful to use speculation methods that have stood the test of the time historically: plus methods that make money regardless of the direction of the markets.

3. *Thinking that overtrading can bring more profits.* Overtrading doesn't improve any statistics, especially when the extant market situation isn't favourable to your trading methodology. Rather than doing

that, you may think of temporarily suspending a certain trading approach until the market conditions become favourable to it. The time of favourable conditions is recognized based on expertise and experience. Another key is to make sure that there's no reason not to trade a particular setup. This ensures that we enter a position based only on our logical entry rules, not on irrational emotions.

4. *Thinking that your education and knowledge in other field can help you in trading.* I know speculators who were very good at other things but who are now grappling desperately with the markets. Bill Gates, who's very successful in the computer world, was recently beaten at a chess game by a chess champion. John McAfee was successful as a software engineer and programmer, but failed as an investor. Your expertise in one field doesn't automatically translate into success in another field. Someone who is successful as a TV superstar may fail as a politician. No matter your level of education or degree of expertise in another field, you'll need to learn the art of successful trading.

Weigh the Consequences

There are consequences for suicidal and safe trading principles and therefore, you would do well to weigh the consequences before you allow your mind to mislead or lead you. Testing a method in real market conditions is more preferable and more agreeable. When a good method doesn't work, we patiently control our risk and wait for the time when the conditions in the market are favourable to it again. The easiest trading methodologies are also the most profitable.

This chapter ends with the quote below:

"When I gave up trading due to frustration and losses. I realised the markets didn't beat me, I beat myself. The classic Jesse Livermore line. I firmly believe that most, if not all of trading over a longer time frame is psychological." – Larry Tentarelli

Chapter 30: What You Need to Know about Strategies Accuracy

AUDCHF

"Markets change continuously. Therefore, I am constantly searching for trading setups that may improve my trading." – Christian Lukas

One of the most important aspects of a strategy is its accuracy percentage. High accuracy is more preferable than low accuracy, although it must be coupled with positive expectancy. A trader whose strategy is only 25% accurate can end up winning if they uses an RRR of 1:5, small sizes and runs their profits. This is something that requires maturity and patience. On the other hand, a trader whose strategy is 75%+ accuracy can end up blowing his portfolio when they uses a worse expectancy like risking $20 to gain $2, doesn't use stops, runs losses indefinitely and uses big sizes.

Having said this, why would most traders still find trading so challenging despite the fact that they use stops and optimal lot sizes? The answers are not far-fetched.

You need to know that the position sizes for huge portfolios aren't the same as the position sizes for small portfolios. Traders who speculate on small accounts would be frustrated when they try to follow the trend. Trend-following is good, but it requires patience, discipline and ability to handle long losing periods. That's why it's better done on huge portfolios. The overall accuracy of strategies that follow the line of least resistance is so low, especially now that false breakouts are no longer a curiosity and sustained trending moves are rather rare. Such are today's markets.

The retail trader finds it difficult to increase their portfolio balance because they use strategies that have low accuracy in most cases. One way to drastically reduce the difficulty is to look for ways to increase your strategy accuracy. Accuracy of 40-50% is certainly better than an accuracy of 25-35%.

This is a fact of trading: when your accuracy is high, it is easier for you to recover your losses and move ahead. When your accuracy is low, recovery of losses is more difficult. The wider a take profit level is, as compared to a stop loss level, the more difficult it is for the take profit level to be hit. The tighter a take profit level is, as compared to a stop loss level, the easier it is for the take profit level to be hit. A tighter take profit level makes sense when strategy accuracy is high, because the stop loss level would be even tighter and the positive expectancy incorporated into the system would be rational.

This is another fact: the higher the accuracy of a system, the less frequent and the more fleeting its losing periods are likely to be. The lower the accuracy of a system, the more frequent and the more protracted its losing periods will be. A trading method whose accuracy is 30% will usually lose more than 20 trades in a row when a losing period materializes; whereas a trading method whose accuracy is about 50% will usually lose less than 15 trades when a losing period materializes. The higher the accuracy, the fewer the losses in a losing period.

We tend to gain money in markets, but we give some of it back during a losing period. Someone says it's not easy to keep money that's made from the markets. By letting profits run and hoping for a target to be hit, we sometimes end up giving back some of our profits, but we want to give back as little as possible. We do this by using small lot sizes, increasing our accuracy, using a rational RRR that's commensurate with the rate of accuracy and temporarily stopping trading after a weekly or monthly drawdown limit has been reached.

Conclusion

The retail trader would do well to look for a strategy that has a higher accuracy, so that the trading experience can be easier and losing periods reduced and more short-lived. Please learn from your past mistakes and adjust your trading style accordingly. When a good football team gets defeated, they learn a lesson. When they win, they also learn a lesson. This is one of the factors that improve their performances in spite of recent failures. This is also true of trading.

This chapter ends with the quote below:

"I have traded now for 13 years and I still have yet to have a year where my winning percentage is over 50 per cent. I posted a 100 trade experiment in 2008 where my win/loss was 48.32 per cent yet the account grew 57.47 per cent." – Adam Jowett

Chapter 31: I Want to Learn Forex but there are Hindrances

GBP CHF

"When you're in love with a market, it shows… in your trading account." – **Old Trader**

It's no longer news that Forex markets are full of opportunities. Sure, there are challenges, but once you learn what it takes to overcome those challenges and become consistently successful, then the opportunities in the markets can bring you rewards. Why do some people feel reluctant to try Forex markets? It's because they think success in the markets isn't easy.

Success in other fields is also not an easy thing. More than 12 years ago, a young woman told me she wanted to become an actress. Obviously, she was dreaming of becoming a celebrity, thinking of the glamor, fame, benefits and riches that are being enjoyed by successful actors and actresses. I only advised her to weigh all the pros and cons of what she wanted to do.

Within a short time she joined a local theatre group and began practicing with them. Several days later, she followed them to a film location. That was when she was exposed to the dark sides of the local film industry: instant privation. This also included paling into insignificance when compared to veteran actors/actress on the location. She saw that her chances of becoming an instant celebrity were very slim. What she dreamed of didn't come as quickly as she'd previously imagined. She thought she would join the industry and quickly become a star; but the reality was different.

When I later saw her, I asked how her about her experience with her new career. She told me the dismal things she faced, including having to work hard without any financial compensation. She swore never to go into the movie industry again and she stood by her promise. Perhaps she could have eventually realised her dreams if she'd pressed on for as long as it would have taken her.

Can you see how this true story relates to trading? Nothing good in life is easy to achieve. Sadly, there are many people who are interested in Forex, but because of one flimsy excuse or another, they keep on postponing the experience that has the potential to bring them financial reward.

Flimsy Excuses

Some have tried everything they think they can do, without attaining any success. They may now threaten that if the new course or strategy that they want to purchase doesn't work, they'll never trade again. As Philip Yancey says, a truly paranoid person organizes his or her life around a common perspective of fear. Anything that happens feeds that fear. The fact is that such people have really lost interest in the markets. While it's wise to learn from the past, we shouldn't live in the past.

Some think that they're currently facing serious expenses and therefore they'll have to wait till next year before they can start learning/trading. The fact is that there's no guarantee that their expenses will be reduced next year.

Some say they want to learn everything they need to know about trading, including taking any courses and reading any books they can find. They think they can't start until they've done that. The fact is that they have yet to learn anything or read any books. If they're yet to do it, will they ever be able to do it at all?

Some think they can learn trading by trial and error. This is possible, but time-consuming and circuitous. They may think they can become a market wizard at will. Then, what stops them from becoming a market wizard?

You may think you can only trade when you're less busy. Do you work only when you're less busy? Trading is a serious business; it's not for those who are less busy.

You may think you can't trade because your family doesn't support you. You may want to think of how to win their support. Maybe if they know and appreciate the truth and realities of trading, they would support you. The way we view our circumstances is more important than the circumstances themselves.

If you say you don't want to trade now, but put it off for the future, you may have forgotten that ephemeral wishes don't mean anything. Anyone who doesn't have the time for trading can't trade. Anyone that doesn't have resources to trade can't trade. We worry so much about protecting ourselves that we fail to step up. These are facts.

Conclusion

What you can do today, don't postpone till tomorrow. The best time to do anything is now. Make your decision and learn how to approach the markets as rationally as possible. There are numerous ways to make money in the markets – just as there are numerous traders in the markets.

The quote below ends the chapter:

"We are all different and there are many ways to win in the markets – the important thing is to develop your own best method." – Charles E. Kirk

Chapter 32: Emotions that Differentiate between Winners and Losers

EUR CAD

"After placing the orders, we leave the rest to the market forces." – Sam Evans

Good traders make a new trade regardless of the outcome of the last trade. However, rookies often allow irrational emotions to guide their actions when they are making trading decisions. Why are some traders always frustrated while others play the markets happily? Let's look at some cogent examples.

1. The bad trader is afraid to make a new trade because of the fear that it may lose. This fear comes regardless of the fact that the setup may be flawless and there's no reason not to trade the setup. On the other hand, as long as the entry criteria are met and there's no reason not to enter the trade, the expert wouldn't hesitate to take the trade.

2. The bad trader tends to be fatalistic in outlook, thinking that trading is a scam or that permanent success isn't attainable. On the other hand, there are more than enough proofs that trading success is possible, plus permanent success. The expert always keeps their chin up. When facing roll-downs, the expert knows it's a fleeting experience.

3. While there is no reason not to trade a setup, the bad trader feels that a trade setup needs much more time to consider before an execution is made. They wants lots of confirmation and guarantee before opening a trade, without knowing that one can trade the best setup and still lose.

4. I was doing it before; I used to check several different websites for fundamental, sentimental and technical confirmation before I took a trade. I wanted to be sure that most pundits were saying the same thing before I took the plunge. Needless to say, I still lost in spite of my painstaking efforts. The expert trader is satisfied with the limited information they has access to.

We don't need to look for complicated analysis or think that there must be a million reasons supporting a setup, before we trade the setup. No matter how beautiful a strategy is, it will still sustain occasional losses. You may think that a particular trading methodology is wonderful, but when it goes through baptism of fire in charting effort, you will see whether it can survive. When risk is under control and the performance is enhanced, the results can then be optimized. When a position first goes in our favour before reverting to the opposite route, we can get out without sustaining any loss on that trade.

Irrational emotions are the reasons why the bad trader is worried while trading, getting frustrated or hesitating to take a trade and eventually missing a great trade or sustaining huge negativity in the markets. Rational emotions are the reasons why the expert trader is calm when trading – being profitable overall.

We evaluate the motion in the markets as money-making opportunities and when we consider the cost of each trade (particularly low spreads), we will appreciate the benefits over time. We will only consider the probability of making money after we also put spreads into consideration. Since there is a cost for each trade, we wouldn't want to overtrade.

The quote below concludes this chapter:

"Strange as it may seem to some, my trading has evolved to a point where I no longer attempt to predict whether stock prices will rise or fall... I found that most of my profits came as result of simply cutting off trades that were either losing or giving up their previous gains; and I could profit from trades entered practically on the flip of a coin." – Chris Ebert

Chapter 33: Being Grateful as Traders

CHF NZD

"Education is incredibly important for traders. Traders should look to educate themselves as much as they can along their trading journey." – **James Hughes**

As I write this, Thanksgiving Day is around the corner in the USA. Thanksgiving Day is a national holiday celebrated primarily in the United States (on the fourth Thursday of November) and Canada (on the second Monday of October) as a day of giving thanks for the blessing of the harvest and of the preceding year. Several other places around the world observe similar celebrations.

The essence of this holiday is to give thanks. In trading also there are many things we can give thanks for. We tend to complain and fret over the disadvantages we think we face, without thinking of the advantages we enjoy. When we ponder the blessings we enjoy in our trading career (as well as in life), those seeming disadvantages pale into insignificance.

During my quiet time, many reasons to be thankful as a trader came to my mind. Obviously, traders now enjoy great tools and services that were not available to those who were speculating just a few decades ago. Here are some of the reasons to be thankful. There are many more – I am sure you can think of some of your own.

1. We're grateful for the opportunity to trade and invest our money.

2. We're grateful for good brokers out there who treat their clients fairly.

3. We're grateful for fund managers who help us make profits by managing our funds.

4. We're grateful for great opportunities like copy trading/social trading, winning signals services, etc. which help us make money.

5. We're grateful for regulatory bodies that regulate brokers, financial institutions, etc. They make financial markets safer for us to trade.

6. We're grateful for cutting-edge trading platforms, data feeds and other tools that are available to us.

7. We're grateful for free and paid education materials that are available to us. We enjoy trading education through various means, including books, DVDs, trading rooms, webinars, etc.

8. We're thankful for many career opportunities that are available in the world of trading.

9. We're grateful for winning trading systems and software – manual, semi-automated and automated strategies that are at our disposal. There are many strategies out there that work.

10. We're thankful for those analytical tools and indicators that are available to us. These things help us to analyse the markets objectively.

11. We're thankful for the fact that trading is a fantastic life-style. We can trade anywhere in the world as long as we have access to a good internet connection.

12. We're thankful that the markets don't discriminate on the basis of nationality, gender, religion, education background, race, tribe, colour, etc. The markets are a level playing field, offering anyone an equal opportunity to be successful irrespective of the aforementioned factors.

13. We're grateful that there are many good trading coaches the world over. They help us master various aspects of trading psychology, risk management, positions sizing, trading systems, chart patterns, trend cycles, etc. These coaches are selfless and altruistic individuals who love to help struggling traders. As for me, when the going was tough and I wanted to quit, I was inspired by successful coaches who made me realise that there are people who are making consistent profits and that I could be successful too.

14. We're thankful for the riches and financial freedom the markets proffer. Many people have made billions of dollars as traders and some of them are among the richest individuals on this planet. You may not become a billionaire (or even a millionaire), but you can become financially free and live a fulfilled life. I define financial freedom as being able to meet your basic needs and still save money for future use.

15. We're grateful for the availability of positive expectancy – which makes us make money regardless of occasional losses. If there were someone who can't lose in the markets, that person would soon have all the money in the world. We do the right things to get the right results. The secret to trading success is in controlling your losses and adding to your winners.

16. We're grateful that the markets don't offer short-cuts to lasting success. More haste in trading is equal to less speed. Short-cuts are very dangerous. Those who take short-cuts are trying to dodge realities, but realities will face them eventually.

17. We're grateful for the movement and liquidity present in the markets. Super rich individuals don't seek to double their portfolios overnight. Instead, they seek slow and steady returns (which translate into great wealth over time). Retracements in the markets can be played by any trader, since they reflect smoothing of positions by large financial establishments. These can cause

contrarian movements in the markets, which are sometimes called significant rallies or dips.

18. We're thankful that we're free moral agents who can choose what our fate will be. Being active in the markets is a matter of interest and choice. When you're interested in something, no-one needs to beg you or persuade you constantly before you do it. You are even willing to spend your time, resources and energy in order to master what you are interested in. But if you aren't interested in something, you won't do it no matter how much noise is made about it, even if you're persuaded again and again.

The list can go on… The tools and services we enjoy as traders ought not to be taken for granted.

Conclusion

We wish Americans a peaceful, blissful and rewarding Thanksgiving Day celebration. At the same time, we are grateful for wonderful opportunities the markets offer us. Yes, there are many reasons to be grateful as traders. When you taste success in your trading career, you'll be hooked and as such, you'd do well to strive for permanent success, not temporary success. May you become a successful trader.

I end this chapter with the quote below:

"Remember, trading from your highest and best self is all that matters to getting your desired trading results." – Dr Woody Johnson

Chapter 34: Traders, Don't Be Like Mr. Geoffrey!

CADAUD

"Anyone who has been involved in the markets has been humbled and respects the fact that this is not an easy game no matter how successful we have already been or how much experience we have." – Charles E. Kirk

About four years ago, Mr. Geoffrey (not his real name) came to me and said he wanted to learn Forex trading. I explained to him that training would take some months because there were crucial aspects of this business that people tended to ignore and we would need to work on those areas.

The training began. Initially, Geoffrey showed interest, but as time went on, he lost patience. He told me that since he knew how to buy, sell, close trades and handle basic operations of trading platforms, he didn't want to waste time with further training. He confessed that he had just purchased some semi-automated trading software which would make him rich very quickly. He showed me the historical results of the strategy as published by the vendors – 4,000% returns in one year!

I tried to caution him against greed, but he thought I was a doubting Thomas who wanted to discourage him from speedy attainment of financial freedom. I was too conservative for him. Geoffrey took a high-interest loan of $5,000 and started trading with it, using that semi-automated strategy. He constantly let me know how his trading was. I saw that he was risking 20% per trade and I warned him against that, telling him that 1% risk per trade would be OK instead.

"I want to pay my kids' school fees," he retorted.

He was able to pay the school fees that week. He even made an additional $120,000 within the next two months and was therefore lucky enough to pay back the loan with the interest on it. His plan was to raise the remaining balance to $1,000,000 before he withdrew everything. I was jealous of his achievement; I began to feel like a fool with the so-called trading beliefs I held on to.

Without mincing words, Dr Woody Johnson says there are traders who have good market knowledge, a good plan and good money management but fail to keep their commitments and follow-through with the plan. I discovered that Geoffrey didn't use stops; he preferred to run negative trades until they came back to entry prices. The strategy he was using had stop loss recommendations included in it, but he ignored those recommendations. I warned him against his failure to use stops.

"Come off it, man. Stops are for chickens," he replied.

I ceased giving him advice.

One day, he messaged me on Skype, asking me what went wrong with the British economy since the Cable (a term used for the GBP/USD currency pair rate) was dropping like a stone. I replied that I knew that kind of drop was normal, so I didn't bother to wonder what caused it. He said nothing in return.

At times, the markets may show sensitivity to fundamental figures and move accordingly; at times, the markets may ignore the fundamentals. After a few days the Cable was still dropping. He messaged me again on Skype, asking me this question: "Should I close the trade?"

I didn't know the trade he was talking about, neither did I advised him to open the trade. So, why would I advise him to close the trade? He opened the trade himself and he should be responsible for the outcome of the trade. His position size was suicidal; plus his trade management technique was dangerous. I didn't respond to his question.

Later I began to empathize with Geoffrey. I was aware that something was wrong with his trading, so I decided to visit him. I found him yelling at his hen.

"You unfortunate hen! You've been incubating your eggs for over 40 days without hatching them. Your mates hatch theirs within 21 days, but you are here showcasing your uselessness. If you want to hatch your eggs, hatch them quickly. If you're not ready to hatch, get out of my sight!"

Geoffrey was extremely bitter as a result of the adverse conditions affecting his trading capital and he was talking it out on the poor hen. He chased the hen away.

As I entered Geoffrey's trading room, I saw that his account was down by -$100,000. He'd previously raised it to +$180,000. He became overconfident and began to risk 30% per trade (without stop loss). He had a few positions that were in favour of the Cable because his semi-automated strategy generated a 'buy' signal. The rally that acted as the cause of the 'buy' signal was a mere rally that trapped the bulls before the currency pair assumed a significantly long-term downtrend.

As I was watching the chart, another fundamental figure affecting the GBP was released. The effect aided the continuation of the downtrend. The market, which had dropped by over 800 pips already, dropped by another 150 pips. Geoffrey suffered.

I was unable to say anything – I felt very sorry for him.

Eventually, Geoffrey closed his positions. The new available balance was less than $1,500. At least he was able to avoid a margin call, wasn't he?

I won't mention the consequences Geoffrey faced as a result of his foolishness.

Like some long trades at the time, the bullish gains quickly evaporated. However, while Geoffrey was badly affected, certain traders have learned how to survive that kind of price action; they've even learned how to make money from that.

This chapter ends with this quote:

"As dedicated as I became, it was not until I was able to both profit and protect my gains that I considered myself a successful trader." – Chris Ebert

Chapter 35: CHF Pairs Volatility – a Blessing and a Curse

USD CAD

"It's futile to call the trade before it happens. One can never know beforehand if a trade is going to be a day trade, a short term trade of days or weeks or a long term trade of weeks up to months. Every trade develops from the embryonic stage of the smallest form on the smallest time scale." – **Dirk Vandycke**

How It Started

On September 2011, the Swiss National Bank (SNB) made a decision to put a peg at the 1.2000 level on EURCHF. They did so because they wanted to stabilize the export industry and the whole economy. It meant that EUR wasn't allowed to reach parity with CHF, unlike other CHF pairs. That previous support level was referred to as a great floor and the SNB would keep on purchasing vast amounts of euros to preclude it from depreciating against Swiss Francs.

In 2011, EURCHF was below the level 1.2000. In fact, EURCHF plummeted by more than 2,800 pips that year, reaching a low of 1.0069. After the peg was effected, the cross jumped upwards above the level 1.2000.

In 2012, the price became very weak, but it was unable to close below the level at 1.2000. Any time the price went below the level, it would jump above the level again.

In 2013, the price was able to trade upwards noticeably, owing to the strength of the euro. The price was able to move upwards by over 500 pips, reaching a high of 1.2648.

In 2014, the price trended downwards in a slow and steady manner until it reached the floor at 1.2000 again at the end of that year. Many saw this as a peerless opportunity to buy EURCHF cross.

EURCHF then looked like 'an unfair' market in which everybody could make money. It was like a market in which everybody could harness huge gains and certain lovers of risk might be willing to risk a huge part of their portfolios. Many thought it was stupid go short on EURCHF, since there was a 'guarantee' that the cross would eventually go up, just like interest rates in some developed countries, which some thought had nowhere to go except upwards. Some didn't even know that interest rates could be made negative. The only thing that could render the scenario useless was when the peg was removed – which the SNB was unwilling to do then.

15 January 2015 – Magnificent Earthquakes in the Markets

Nevertheless, it was getting more and more expensive for the SNB to defend the peg. A central bank would need very deep pockets to keep on doing that for a long time. The SNB reserves increased to a record high and the outlook on the euro was becoming more and more gloomy. It was clear that holding onto that floor was illogical. On 15 January 2015, the SNB suddenly removed the peg and decreased the interest rate further into the negative territory. The trading world was taken by surprise. Some traders made huge profits and losses. Only those who didn't trade CHF pairs were not seriously affected.

USDCHF dropped by 2,800 pips.
EURCHF dropped by 3,300 pips
GBPCHF dropped by 4,300 pips
CADCHF dropped by 1,500 pips

CHFJPY rallied by 6,900 pips
NZDCHF dropped by 1,500 pips
AUDCHF dropped by 1,500 pips

These moves were unprecedented! A daily candle was as long as a human arm! While it is normal for a pair/cross to experience a directional movement of thousands of pips within several days, weeks or months, it's not normal for a pair/cross to move so much in a single day. The market is like a rubber band; if it moves too far in one direction, you should expect it to snap back in the opposite direction. Thus there were significant corrections on that day alone.

Neither the SNB nor the markets can be blamed for this: a central bank has the right to do what they want with their currency. In addition, the markets conditions that brought losses to some are the same conditions that brought profits for others. Good risk managers suffer negligible loss when caught on the wrong side of the market and they make commendable gains when they're caught on the right side.

Lessons for Gamblers

I know someone who made a profit of 7,000,000 euros in two hours. Someone who funded his account with $100 and was using 0.1 lots made 2,600% returns in a single day. Someone who funded his account with $1,000 and traded with 0.5 lots came home from work and saw an account balance of over $10,000. Many brokers now need to pay their clients gargantuan amounts of profits.

If you made huge profits here, like several hundreds of percentage of profits, it was only a matter of luck; and no trader can experience permanent success based on pure luck. Good traders are those who survive adverse market conditions, not just those who make big money from the markets.

On the other hand, many traders received margin calls or lost most part of their portfolios. Imagine someone using 60.0 lots on a

1,000,000 pounds account. Needless to say, the money was lost immediately. Certain brokers were badly affected (though most were unaffected). I deeply empathize with those who were badly affected.

I was also affected, for I was holding two long positions on EURCHF and NZDCHF, but I suffered only -1.2% losses in total. My loss should have been only 1% on the two trades, but you know, slippage. Stops will forever be our life insurance policy. If you follow the advice of those who don't use stops, your losses can't be their responsibility.

Do you remember the 6 May 2010 Flash Crash? Do you remember the earthquake in Japan, which occurred on 11 March 2011, plus the nuclear disaster that followed? Do you know the effects they had on the markets? Do you know how traders were affected and what happened following massive drops in prices? These should serve as lessons against the Gambler's Fallacy. Unfortunately, many people seemed not to learn their lesson.

Overconfidence is definitely not a good thing.

As you can see, whether you trade with fundamental or technical analysis or combine both, you don't know what the market will do next and you can't be always right. Even those who foresaw that the peg would be removed didn't know when exactly it would be. When things go wrong, only risk control will help you, not your knowledge of technical or fundamental things. It's better to focus on what we can control – our winners and losers.

It's not the best idea to sacrifice permanent success for short-term greed. Those who appear stupid by doing the right things will eventually be proven to be prudent.

When I recommend the risk of 0.5% per trade, most people ignore me. In fact, you'd hardly see someone using only 0.1 lots on a $20,000 account or 0.5 lots on a $100,000 account. They think it's too illogical and conservative, playing down my warning that the safety of our portfolios are more important that the profits we want to make. Large losses are extremely difficult to recover and therefore, they should be avoided at all costs. The most guaranteed setup in the world can't make me risk more than 0.5% on any of my future trade.

I've been an advocate of permanent success, but it can't be achieved by those who use large position sizes. Leverage isn't a problem, but an irrational use of leverage is the problem. Leverage is a boon to risk managers who know how to control their losses and profits.

Next Directions on CHF Pairs

The SNB might still try to keep the CHF undervalued and they may explore another means of doing so. Opportunities to go long arose when prices declined towards ridiculously abnormal levels. These kinds of movements in a single day are extremely spectacular and therefore, current CHF pairs' prices are bound to get corrected in the long run and things will return to normal in a matter of weeks. For instance, when USDCHF dropped like a stone, EURUSD ought to spike skywards, since they are negatively correlated in a normal condition. The latter was not affected and both pairs cannot remain bearish for a long time (and the dollar is strong in its own right). USDCHF moved upwards by over 1,900 pips for the rest of 2015 (from the January 2015 low of 0.8246). Looking at the big picture, USDCHF has largely consolidated so far since then.

These kinds of markets offer unique opportunities to assume contrarian positions. At the end of 15 January 2015, I went long on EURCHF, USDCHF, AUDCHF, NZDCHF, GBPCHF and CADCHF (selling short CHFJPY), using a position size of 0.1 lots for each $20,000. I targeted 500 pips on each trade. I held these long positions for weeks or months – until all the targets were met. I didn't make use of breakeven or trailing stops this time around because I wanted to create enough leeway for the high volatility in the markets, while I enjoyed the free ride.

The bearish pair and crosses cannot remain bearish forever. The CHF markets were expected to correct themselves gradually until things became normal. As some basked in the euphoria of windfall and others licked their wounds, we shouldn't forget the lessons we learned from the CHF pairs volatility, which were a blessing and a curse.

This chapter is ended with the quote below:

"If you trade at a size that's nearly meaningless, there will be very little emotions involved. However, if you are taking on big risks you will make emotional mistakes." – Dave Landry

Chapter 36: You Can Enjoy Trading

GBP JPY

"Traders produce success, trading systems do not!" – Dr Van K Tharp

Have you ever felt as I did when I was a novice? Sometimes trading turns out to be a far cry from our dreams. Painful results can seem to drag on endlessly and it can be hard to see a way out or a way to endure. Needless to say, those who endured in the past now enjoy trading and the benefits that come from it. How can you enjoy trading? Here are some of the ways.

Cultivate a Positive View of Trading

We can view trading as a means to an end. If you're able to acquire what you need as a trader, then your trading is doing what it's supposed to do. Successful traders love the feeling they have after a long period of trading. They may have worked hard to achieve success and their work may have gone unnoticed by others – but they know they've accomplished something. That thing is a profit.

Apply Yourself to Trading Mastery

Of course, you don't become a skilled trader automatically, and not many people cherish engaging themselves in what they've not mastered. Maybe that's the reason why many don't like trading, for they simply haven't put forth enough effort to become good at it.

Focus on How Your Trading Activity Can Benefit Others

Avoid the trap of thinking only about how much money you can make for yourself, but think about how others also benefit from your trading. The world of trading is a unique ecosystem in which you, your family, the broker, the liquidity provider, etc. benefit and can't do without one another. Think of how those who need help can be helped when you become a rich trader.

Truly, when we strive hard and reach a good level of competence in trading, we can provide for ourselves and our family and we can also help those who are in need. So trading can make us experience the happiness of giving.

Go the Extra Mile

Rather than simply reaching a level of competence in trading, look for ways to become a super trader. No matter your level of expertise, there'll always be room for improvement. Set quarterly or annual goals for yourself. Challenge yourself to trade better and with more maturity. When you do this, you're more likely to enjoy trading. This is because you're in control of your mindset and actions. You're doing well because you want just that, not because you're forced into doing that.

Keep Trading in its Proper Place

Profitable speculation is admirable, yet we do well to remember that there's more to life than speculation. Although it's a noble idea to dedicate yourself to trading success, you need to think of other important things in life. What are these? These are your family and friends and other activities that matter to your spiritual and physical health.

Joe Ross, Van K. Tharp, Anne-Marie Baiynd (quoted below) and many others are examples of persons with balanced trading ethics. They've worked hard to achieve success in trading and they've left great impression on their clients because of the quality of their services. But in the end, when the job is done, they know how to leave trading behind temporarily and focus on their family and other things they cherish. And you know what? They're among the happiest traders on this planet.

Conclusion

When trading seems difficult as a result of a lack of expertise, who among us doesn't need to work on our endurance? In order to face the ongoing challenges in the markets, we need the kind of determination, patience and inner peace that only conservative risk control and sane position sizing can give us.

The quote below ends this chapter:

"Our success is not about how much knowledge we have, but how we make decisions when our senses are heightened by fear or anxiety." – Anne-Marie Baiynd

Chapter 37: When a Good Strategy Is Losing Money – Part 1

EUR JPY

"But in the market any price is always history. It's the price of the last transaction, holding no guarantee for even the nearest future." – Dirk Vandycke

What do you do when a good trading system, whose historical results have been satisfactory, gets into a losing streak? Good strategies lose now and then, and then gain now and then. Losing streaks are alternated by winning streaks, and what you can do is to minimize your losses in losing periods, controlling the drawdowns on your accounts. This is done so that your capital will be intact when a winning period comes around. This is a reality of trading and there's no way around it. Yet it doesn't preclude you from being consistently profitable in spite of occasional drawdowns.

People who are rational in other fields tend to be irrational when trading. They don't know that trading is just any other business in life. There's no strategy on earth (and there'll never be one) which doesn't experience drawdowns. No matter what trading approach you have adopted, there'll be periods when the price actions are against you.

We're happy when we make money, without giving any thoughts to how we control our emotions when we lose. We're able to remain calm during losing streaks, providing that we're willing to do that. Let's think about a system that wins about 65% of the time. That means we may have about 35 losing trades out of 100. When you buy such a system, you can lose the first 10 or 20 trades (or even more) in a row. Then you conclude that the system is trash. You don't know that the system could soon start winning many trades in a row.

Trading has to with probabilities and profits are analysed over a long period of time – not over a short period of time. When about 100 trades are analysed, then you would see the merit of a good strategy. Trading should be treated like an enterprise: losses being the cost of running the enterprise and profits being the reward you gain from your venture.

Our society is rife with perfectionism tendency, and that's why there are many people who criticize everything, expecting too much of other people while they themselves aren't perfect. Those who do well in life are probably correct less than half of the time, yet mistakes are often ridiculed. Perfectionism has no place in profitable market speculation. You have to realise that one needs to stick to a positive expectancy system even in a period of losses, for it will soon be in a winning period. However, most people dump such a system and look for another fool-proof one. The truth, however, is that another 'fool-proof' system that has good results in the past would also experience drawdowns. Would you then dump such a system again? You might trash the new system and look for yet another one.

For you to be called a super trader, you have to stick to a good strategy throughout its vicissitudes. Profitable speculation in the market needs perseverance, rules and determination. You get rich slowly, not quickly. Success comes at cost – it requires effort and doggedness. Keep a log of your trades and look for ways to optimize the system.

Should you disagree with this, you may want to go from one trading method to another, for life. Otherwise, you may want to master a good trading method and stick to it for life. Should you prefer the latter, you may eventually reach financial freedom. A good system makes money eventually, but you'll need to be faithful to it, which is something that irrational traders don't want to do.

You make money when a market moves. A fast-moving market like Forex is ideal, since you make money when the move is in your favour. But you don't make money when the move is against you. Please take risk and money management seriously. This is your life insurance in the markets. All traders experience negativity, but good traders deal with negativity sensibly. You need to risk only 1%, or better, less per trade. You need to make sure that you don't go down less than 4% or 5% in total. When the position sizes are too big, it is difficult to control emotions.

The most important thing in trading is not to lose one's capital. We trade not to lose, and that's the only way to prepare for slow and steady growth when the time comes. Only effective risk managers can survive in the markets indefinitely.

We learn much more from losing trades, and we learn very little from profitable trades. Therefore, it's what we learn from losing trades that make us better traders. In other words, loses are the catalyst that enables us to hone our trading skills.

This chapter ends with the quote below:

"Without a plan and money management the best setups in the world are useless." – Dave Landry

Chapter 38: When a Good Strategy Is Losing Money – Part 2

CAD NZD

"When I was 20 to 25 years younger, every move in the markets would make me excited. By the mid-90s, I got my emotions under control. I learned to focus on eliminating risk on the front end, so that I would have fewer problems on the back end." – **David J. Merkel**

Mr. Liam (not his real name) was attracted to a trading strategy software as it was being pitched. The two-year historical results were amazing, as shown by the vendor of the software. The results showed a historical hit rate of 70%, but the software was very expensive. In order to purchase the software, Mr. Liam had to pay in four instalments. After that, he was able to get the software.

However, Liam lost money with the strategy and he got the vendor arrested.

Because Liam was a good reader – reading many trading article and magazines – he discovered that there were successful traders. Since he was inspired by testimonies from super traders, he continued working to improve his knowledge.

When he attained some level of competence, he put the strategy to test again and saw that the strategy was wonderful. He realised that he himself, not that strategy, was responsible for his loss. He felt sorry for the strategy vendor and as a result of that, he visited the vendor and tendered his heartfelt apology. He even gave the vendor a cash gift of $1,000.

A great strategy can't work for a suicide trader.

The Power of Choice

Anyone who says they can never lose is an accomplished liar. Anyone who says their strategy doesn't lose is also a distinguished fabricator. Losses are a blessing in disguise because they're the secrets that help us become better traders. When you lose money with a good strategy, after being faithful to it, it's up to you to decide whether to quit or continue.

There was a legendary trader who made and lost fortunes in the markets. We have much to learn from such a great trader, so that we know what's behind his success and can imitate him. We also want to know the cause of his failure so that we can avoid that in our trading. The truth about trading is timeless and it will forever be. Humans drive the markets and as such, various human emotions are reflected in price actions. When things go wrong, we want to make sure that the effects on our portfolios are minimal.

Successful traders lost in the past. But they continued until they reached a stage where they started making money effortlessly. When they were losing, some people tried to discourage them, thinking they had their best interest in heart. If you allowed yourself to be discouraged because of the current fleeting losing streak, then in future you'll only be green with envy when you hear how much successful traders are being paid.

Superstars, celebrities, politicians, athletes, etc. have always faced ignominious defeats now and then in their careers. The greatest role models accepted defeats in the past, but they moved on. Similarly, the greatest role models accept defeats today and they move on. Their transitory failures were the secrets of the enviable breakthroughs they enjoyed later.

Check the stories of very great people in various walks of life, past and present. You'll understand what I'm talking about.

Super traders today refused to be discouraged when things were tough, when their friends and folks were asking them to try another 'safe' ways to earn livelihood. The other 'safe' alternatives that many members of the public prefer to trading are the major reason why more and more members of the public are getting poorer and poorer. Those who allowed themselves to be discouraged paid a heavy price for their short-sightedness.

The Inevitable Experiences

It's easy to criticize others while we are being blinded to our imperfection. Everyone thinks they're right, until the markets prove them wrong. We would do ourselves a great favour by focusing on our own weaknesses and working on them: instead of focusing on other people's weaknesses.

All traders will experience negativity. You can continue to experience negativity, irrespective of what you do, until you start asking what's really wrong with your life. At this stage, you'll doubt your possibility of becoming a profitable market speculator. Yes, all traders experience negativity and sadly, that's the stage where most others quit. No wonder then that few people can share testimonies to the possibility of everlasting success in the markets.

Very few traders move beyond the stage where they lose, no matter what they do. Indeed, very few people will rise up and continuing struggling again, after they've been floored by the markets. You must master yourself before you master the markets. Bad trading results are an evidence of personality flaws in you and good trading results are evidence that you've controlled those flaws.

The few people who rise up to struggle again will inevitably reach a stage when they start making money effortlessly and consistently. These are the people that the public call "market wizards," "super traders," "pros," "expert speculators," "gurus," "witches," "mad geniuses," etc. The public think something is special about them, but these people know that there's nothing special about them. They're consistently profitable because of their many years of experience, plus their winning speculation principles have been practiced again and again until they become their second nature. You think they're smarter, more brilliant, more fortunate, more intelligent and more innovative. Nevertheless, they think they're no better than you. What makes the difference is that they decided to continue fighting for success at the stage that most others quit.

We're given the power of choice to use for future glory or future regret. Even if we have challenges in the markets, why can't we seek help from professional traders and coaches? If you got a persistent toothache, you go to a dentist. Then why not seek help from a trading professional when you've a challenge?

The quote below ends this chapter:

"You also need to be able to trade a setup even when it is profitable. By that I mean that you need to stick to it throughout all the ups and downs. After all, it takes several tries with some setups for the trade to work. Until it does, you must be able to continue trading with confidence." – Ruediger Born

Chapter 39: Forex Trading versus Binary Options – Part 1

AUDUSD

"Nobody can predict the future. A Harvard PhD and a high school dropout have equal skills at prophecy." – James Altucher

It's no longer a secret that the Forex market is the biggest and the fastest-growing market in the world. It's also not a secret that the majority of Forex traders end up sustaining negativity, simply because they don't know what can really make them profitable, or they know but fail to do it.

As a result of this, many people have been singing the praises of binary options* as a wonderful alternative, casting aspersions on Forex. They think it's easier to make money from binary options than from Forex. Is that correct? What are binary options? Investopedia defines it as a type of option in which the payoff is structured to be either a fixed amount of compensation if the option expires in the money, or nothing at all if the option expires out of the money. The success of a binary option is thus based on a yes/no proposition, hence 'binary.'

'Binary' means 'two parts,' since a speculator will only need to predict that an instrument would rise above (Call) or fall below (Put) a certain price level in a given day or week. Unlike Forex, in which you essentially trade currencies, binary options traders can trade indices, Forex, stocks and commodities.

Sports, markets and businesses are all zero sum games. Then what about binary options?

Is it possible to make money trading binary options? Is it possible to make money trading Forex?

The answer to both questions is yes… If a binary options trader is much conversant with, say, the oil market, he can make money predicting whether the price will rise or fall above a certain price level in a day or a week.

However, contrary to popular opinion, Forex has certain advantages when compared to binary options. The seeming simplicity of binary options trading – only Call or Put – doesn't mean it's easy for enjoying long-term success.

Forex versus Binary

I'm a living witness to this fact. A trader who uses a system that has only 50% accuracy can survive in Forex, but there is no way they can survive with 50% accuracy when trading binary options. A trader with only 25% accuracy can make money in Forex, but they will quickly crash when approaching binary options with a system that has a hit rate of only 25% accuracy.

I can risk $50 or $100 to target $200 in Forex, but that's never possible with binary options. The risks are always higher than the rewards and that's a worse expectancy. In binary for example, you can risk $100 to gain $50 or $70 or $85 or even $90, but no broker will ever give you a risk-to-reward ratio of 1 to 1, let alone 1 to 2. Forex inherently gives you a risk-to reward ratio of 1 to 10 or 20 or 30, depending on how long you're willing to let your profits run. We can enjoy everlasting success with positive expectancy only.

Let's say a broker allows a reward of $80 for every $100 you risk for each binary prediction, you'll then need to achieve at least 70% accuracy to survive in the long-term. Believe me, this is very hard because the future can't be predicated. With 70% hit rate, you're likely to experience four or five losses in a row with 1,000 trials, and with this, someone with a small account can deplete it before a winning prediction comes around. With rewards that are smaller than risks, chances of long-term survival using 70% accurate systems are slim indeed. Researchers have confirmed that people have trouble surviving with even an 80% hit rate, owing to psychological factors.

In Forex, people have made fortunes with trading systems that have a reliability of around 25%-35%. They do so by following the timeless Golden Rule of trading: Cut your losses short and let your profits run. You can't do that in binary options. You succeed when an average loss is smaller than an average gain, not the other way round.

We enjoy everlasting success as traders because there are many things we can control, save the market itself. We can control risks and manage our trades effectively. But in binary options, you can't control anything, for you're at the mercy of the market forces once a position is triggered.

If a market moves in my favour before going against me, I can eliminate the risk or negativity with a break-even stop, so that a movement against me won't result in negativity. This is not possible with binary options, for you lose your entire stake irrespective of the fact that a selected instrument first moves in your favour before reversing against you. Though some may say that binary makes you win even if an instrument first moves against you and later moves in your favour, before the expiration. This is also true of Forex; a position that is in a negative territory can later turn positive.

I can decide to cut my loss before my stop is hit, so that my loss is limited even more effectively. If I gain, say about 200 pips in a trade, I can lock part of it and ride the move even further. I can even take part of the profit and ride the move further. These things aren't possible with binary options. I'm happy when I see that my losses are smaller than my profits. I know if I traded binary, my stakes would be higher than my rewards. Trading binary options is inherently a negative expectancy game. If other financial markets are zero sum games, the binary options is a minus sum game.

For those who don't agree with the point raised here, only their personal experience after years will prove the point.

Conclusion

I'm not discouraging people from binary options. There are successful binary traders out there, but I've realised that Forex gives me far more freedom to choose my fate in the markets. When you trade a market that you're very good at, you make fewer mistakes and improve your results. Investing in what you're conversant with is essential to your financial well-being. Genuine wisdom is scarce and therefore, success is attainable only when you do what you're good at. That's why I enjoy trading Forex: that's my area of competence.

Please read the quotes above and below and ponder them. They are from Markham Gross.

"A good trader by contrast will be focused on running a repeatable system having positive mathematical expectancy without need or regard for knowing or talking about the future."

"It would be impossible to have gains without some loss along the way. My strategy actually results in more losing trades than winners, which is sometimes shocking to people. We win by keeping losses small."

* Please note that there are differences between regular options and binary options. This chapter addresses Forex and binary options (not regular options, a good investment vehicle). In order to know the difference between binary options and regular options, please see this link: http://www.ibinarytrade.com/whats-the-difference-between-binary-and-regular-options/

Chapter 40: Forex Trading versus Binary Options – Part 2

GBP AUD

Binary Options Myths versus Realities

"To be successful, you must keep in mind that the only way you can continue to operate is to protect your account from a major setback or, worse, devastation. Avoiding large losses is the single most important factor for winning big as a speculator. You cannot control how much a stock rises, but in most cases, whether you take a small loss or a big loss is entirely your choice. There is one thing we can guarantee: if you cannot learn to accept small losses, sooner or later you will take big losses. It is inevitable." – Mark Minervini (Source: Tradersonline-mag.com)

This is just to debunk myths surrounding binary options (also called fixed odds), opening our eyes to facts.

Arguments in Favour of Binary Options

Because of its plausible simplicity, many people are attracted to binary options, thinking that Forex requires a bit of getting used to. In fact, many so-called binary options experts have documented some logical arguments in favour of binary options and to some extent they're partially correct.

Do you think binary options (BO) have some advantages over Forex? OK, let's examine a few advantages the experts claim BO has and see whether the advantages aren't in Forex.

Myth 1

BO is based on time and FX is based on price. Most FX traders overlook time factor in their trading while BO traders are time-conscious.

Reality

The market doesn't care whether you trade it based on price or time. You may enter with a specific timeframe or a specific price in mind, but that doesn't guarantee anything. It will do what it will do without having you in mind, and this can be in your favour or against you, whether you trade BO or FX. You timing may be wrong immediately or later or never. You timing may be correct immediately or later or never. This has little role to play in your success.

Myth 2

BO traders are forced to exit a position in a given timeframe either with a win or a loss. Since they're forced to do this, they have an advantage over FX traders who can refuse to exit a position with a win or a loss because of greed and fear.

Reality

Yes novice FX traders can hold onto losing positions and abort winners, which is a bad trading approach. But disciplined traders cut their losses and give their winners some leeway. Being forced to exit at a given time doesn't make you the richest trader; otherwise, automated systems would be second to none. Being forced to exit always at predetermined levels can't help if your trading approach is bad and the market has an inherent negative expectancy. The discipline you enforce on yourself is much more satisfying than the discipline someone imposes on you.

BO traders suffer the disadvantage of being forced out against their will, though the most important issue is profitability, which still eludes many in spite of being forced out at expiry periods. In FX, we're comfortable exiting at our convenient time. We may continue running a profit in order to maximize it. From 3-11 March 2015, I'd have gained about 500 pips if I had gone long on USDCHF and I let my profit run.

Myth 3

BO helps reduce emotions because risk and reward plus expiry are all fixed and predetermined.

Reality

All traders in all financial markets aren't immune to emotions, so BO is no exception. Permanent success in trading includes a measure of managerial control of our positions. This isn't possible in BO, for you remain helpless once a position is open, waiting for expiry.

Considering the myths and realities above, I'd like to chip in some fallacies some BO traders carry in their heads and the facts about the fallacies.

Higher Accuracy Fallacy

According to one source, BO by its nature requires a greater than win rate as each bet is factored 70%-90% gain against 100% loss. So this means that you need to achieve as a BO trader a win rate above 50% on average 54%-58% to just break even.

The fact is that in the long run no one can achieve more than 50% accuracy. 80%, 90%, 75% etc. hit rates are false in the end. They might be true in hindsight, but not in live markets. Even scalpers who risk 500 USD to gain 2 USD per trade in FX trading would seem to have high hit rates, but this would drop significantly when the hit rates are reduced.

It is a fallacy to think there are computer, automated, custom, alien, astronomical, spiritual, mental, discretionary, fundamental, manual, etc. strategies that enable us to get a hit rate which is higher than 50%. Marketers and novice traders would tell us so, but many people have lost money with systems that are promised to carry very high accuracy because the future can't be predicted. Something that sounds great in theory can fail in practice and what looks like a perfect plan can be overturned by a factor beyond our control.

BO traders are often fooled into believing they can achieve a hit rate of 70% or more permanently. You might as well do that with the toss of a coin endlessly. No matter how good or how complicated your strategy or indicator is, you're guaranteed only 50% hit rate or less in the long run. When tossing a coin endlessly, the share between heads and tails will balance off at 50/50.

Albeit, there can be times when heads will be hit more than tails within several weeks or months (or even years). You get heads ten times and tails twice. Then heads another eight times and tails three times. Then heads nine times and tails four times. This would give you a false impression that you have a trading approach with a high accuracy, without you being aware that it's winning streaks that cause that. On a long-term basis, things would turn the other way and you get levelled at 50% because tails would begin to be hit more than heads (like getting tails nine times and heads twice).

The only way to survive is to make more money in winning periods than you lose in losing periods. Does BO allow this?

Money Management Fallacy

Money management is very important in trading any financial markets, and so BO traders claim they can get ahead with good money management methods. The issue is this: can a good money management method help you in a game in which your risks will always be higher than your rewards? How can you survive in a game in which you'll be paid only 70 or 80 USD for each 100 USD you risk?

If you win you gain 80 USD, but if you lose, you forfeit 100 USD. Does that appeal to you? What money management can you use?

It doesn't matter whether you risk 1% or 0.5% or 2% per trade – you simply gain less than you stake no matter what you do. Money management makes sense only when your losses are smaller than your gains, not the other way round.

Let's say you get paid 90 USD for each 100 USD (because this is the highest the most generous broker can give you) and you place 100 trades in a year.

Let's use 100 trials with 90% payout ratio (most brokers pay only 50%-80% of the capital risked). Let's say you have a capital of about 10,000; assuming the money management is 1% per trade. 100 x 100 = 10,000.

You win 50%

90 USD X 50 = 4,500 USD

You lose 50%

-100 USD X 50 = -5,000 USD

Is this ever logical or rational?

In FX, we can risk 50 USD per trade to gain 200 USD. With this, we can lose 75% of our trades and still make money.

-50 USD X 75 = -3,750 USD (loss)

200 USD X 25 = 5,000 USD (win)

Doesn't this make sense to you?

The Gambler's fallacy

The only way to enjoy longer term success in BO is to use Martingale position sizing methods, which make you double your next stake to cover the previous loss (and this doesn't present any huge edge in itself). Please search for information on the internet in order to find out what Martingale is and how it works.

Martingale isn't ideal for most traders because they don't have enough money. This is a serious problem. Too many traders open accounts with too small funds, and under such circumstances, good money management can't be practiced.

Unfortunately, those who have big accounts either don't understand concepts of excellent position sizing or fail to respect the concepts.

This leads us to the Gambler's fallacy. When you're in a losing streak, you think your chances of winning improve with next positions, since your previous ones are losses. You think the winners are around the corner. Doubling your stakes with each loss increases your negativity and depletes your account quickly.

Maybe after four losing trades, which cost you 2,000 USD, you double your stake to 4,000 USD. You could have the fifth straight loss because you're still in a losing streak.

Even if you wait for four losses in a row before risking 20% of your account to recover the recent losses, you still face a gambler's problem because your next trade could be a loss, and this has nothing to do with what happened to you in the past.

The Grass Is Always Greener
on the Other Side of the Fence

Some hate transport business and some love it. The risks in transport business (accidents, failures, low patronage, losses, problems with authorities, etc.) don't deter some people from doing it because of its rewards. Some who fail at agriculture think sports is better. Some who fail at politics now want to try publishing, whereas publishing has its own challenges. Some who have been disillusioned with salaried jobs now want to try the music industry; whereas it isn't easy to be a celebrity or a promoter. Some who started their business have also seen that remaining profitable isn't easy. ***Certain people don't want to do anything with trading until they're financially down, having exhausted all other alternatives. Is that the right time to become a trader?***

Those who don't make money with CFD believe spread betting is better. Those who hate shares markets consider futures markets. ***Those who have problems with FX think BO is better.***

What do you want to do with your life? What do you want to do for a living? What can you do to put food on your table (or to feed your kids, if you're a parent)? Life's short: only 70-90 years, and some don't even reach that age bracket. A short life is meaningful if one is financially free and is fulfilled.

Caveat

I didn't mean to anger BO traders. BO is good and it offers nice potentials, but people are also blinded to its pitfalls and inherent disadvantages. A business that always makes profits that are bigger than expenses will sometimes go through turbulent times; how much more a business that makes profits that are always smaller than expenses!

If I made a business proposal to you, telling you that your income/profits from the business would be primarily, permanently less than your expenses and other costs of running the business, would you agree to the business proposal? Does that kind of business sound rational to you? Sadly, this is the permanent reality of BO.

It doesn't make sense to run a business in which the costs will always be bigger than income.

I'll trade BO only when brokers start giving us the possibility of getting a reward that is bigger than the risk per trade. However, I sense that this may put them at a disadvantage.

Conclusion

The most exciting thing about the market is its unpredictability. The unpredictability of our trading career isn't always thrilling, however. We devise and strategize. We make trading plans, projections and proposals about what we'd like to see happen to our portfolios, but often they're little more than our best guesses. We have no idea what a day, a week, a month or even a year might bring.

"Why don't you just play around with the idea that you can be wrong and still be successful. Being right or wrong is a meaningless invention of your mind. Instead, what if you just developed a good system and practiced following it? A loss has nothing to do with being wrong. Instead, a loss has everything to do with following your system and not making a mistake…. So what if you just accepted losses when you got them, allowing them to be small losses and let your profits run when you have a good trade? Don't you think that might be a good idea?" – Dr Van K Tharp (Source: Vantharp.com)

Chapter 41: The Travails of the Signals Provider

USD JPY

"No matter how great a setup looks, there's always a chance you can still be wrong... Realise that knowing when not to trade is as important as knowing when to trade. I often joke that we are more wait-ers than trade-ers."

A signals provider is a trading professional who gives buy and sell recommendations to interested clients. This can be through newsletters, email alerts, SMS, auto trading, social trading, etc. In most cases, stop loss levels, take profit levels, exit dates, money management recommendations and so on are included with the signals. While there are trading signals systems that lose money over time, there are also trading signals that win money over time. Unless doctored, historical performances of good signals systems have average winners that are bigger than average losers.

For a strategy to work, it must be followed as recommended. Unfortunately, many clients either add irrelevant rules or do something else that is against the strategy, and they will still put blame on the signals provider. We tend to forget that signals providers aren't gods.

One associate professor, who is also a trading advisor, tells of his experience with clients. When the market conditions are favourable, the clients will be happy and send him their good will. When the market conditions are not favourable, they become sad and send him words of anxiety and hopelessness, as well as questions. When the markets crash further, the clients call, email and send in words of frustration, together with oaths.

Inexperienced traders that trade based on my recommendations hold me in high esteem whenever the strategy is making money. They may even become overconfident. They may add additional positions that are contrary to my recommendations and risk far too large portions of their portfolios, contrary to my suggestions. However, when the signals strategy is experiencing a losing streak – as is normal for all strategies– many people would think I'm stupid. They would even wonder if I am a professional as I claim. They unsubscribe from my services before the signals start making money again.

When new signals aren't sent because the existing market situation precludes the entry criteria from being met, some clients initiate trades of their own. When they gain from such trades, they feel proud of themselves. When they lose money, they blame the signals provider who failed to send signals when they needed them. Such is the travail of the signals provider.

Good traders who follow positive expectancy religiously are sometimes referred to as wise fools. Good traders aren't just those who make money from the markets; they are those who can keep their hard-earned profits and survive terrible losing streaks.

This reminds me of when I was a private tutor (many years ago). Parents hired private tutors to teach their kids at home, with the hope that the teachers are magicians who can perform academic miracles on their kids. You see, there are many factors that contribute to academic failures of children. When a kid fails an exam in spite of the effort of a private tutor, the tutor is the one to blame for the failure, even if they doesn't deserve that. The parents don't usually blame schools, school teachers, the kids, themselves, technology, environment, etc.

Something that sounds perfect in theory may fail in practice. A good strategy that sounds great when analysed will experience occasional drawdowns. Our job is to lose as small an amount as possible during losing streaks and move forward during winning streaks.

Conclusion

For many years, I've been happily engaged in the markets. I've learned that the principles that lead to trading success are logical and simple, yet at the same time a priceless treasure. That's why I appreciate sharing my convictions and wonderful secrets with others. Today I know that success in the market is attainable rather than elusive.

The quote at the beginning of this chapter is from Dave Landryas is the one below:

"With my methodology there will be extended periods where there is nothing to do. Trying to make something happen during these conditions because you need the money will create losses. Also, trends take time to develop."

Chapter 42: What Is the Right Time to Trade?

NZD USD

"Trading success depends on your system, your relationship with yourself and your relationships with others. Your feelings drive all of these components. When I first started, I thought it was all about the system. How silly and naïve I was in those days." – Mike Melissinos

What do you think is the answer to the question asked by the chapter heading? There's no general answer, for it depends on your trading style and approach. Let's take some examples.

A scalper looks for an opportunity to enter the market in the short-term and when the opportunity presents itself, they enters the market immediately, taking advantage of short-term market movements. Some swing traders or positions traders have various entry criteria for opening and closing positions. Some enter immediately the entry criteria are met, while some would wait for the market to close or for the following day before they enter.

Some traders use pending orders to take advantage of certain price actions and once a pending order is filled, trading begins. Some speculators use fundamental events to enter the market as soon as the entry requirements are met and some use fundamental events to project long-term movements.

As you can see, the right time to trade really depends on your trading style and approaches. Once you enter the market by whatever means or criteria you choose, just make sure that you stick to your trade management rules – plus entry and exit rules. Irrational emotions tempt speculators to go against their rules. While it is difficult to control one's temper while driving on a busy road, some have learned to control it while driving. You can control your emotions while trading and therefore, avoid taking actions that you'll later regret.

This chapter ends with the quote below:

"Trading success comes from developing for yourself a good, well thought-out trading plan. That's a plan which is based on your personal needs, strengths, interests, and all of that." – John Forman

Chapter 43: The Greatest Trading Skill in the World

USD AUD

"With every trade or investment there are four possible outcomes. You can have a small win, big win, small loss or big loss. As long as we make sure we eliminate the big loss from happening, we can certainly live with the other three." – Sam Seiden

What's the most important thing every trader can/must do? What's the greatest trading skill in the world?

One market wizard was asked this question and he answered that there are three things you must do:

1. Cut your losses.

2. Cut your losses.

3. Cut your losses.

If you can do these three things, then you may have a chance of becoming a successful trader.

Warren Buffet also has been quoted as saying that there are two most important things you must do:

1. Don't lose your money.

2. Don't forget the rule above.

The market has no respect for your educational background or achievements. It has no respect for your high school diploma or a collection of PhDs. The market doesn't respect your political posts or achievements. The market doesn't respect any strategy you use whatsoever: whether simple or complicated. The market doesn't know whether you're highly experienced or have no experience. The market has no knowledge of your religious background, beliefs and titles. The market has no acknowledgment of your race, tribe, nationality, region, age or gender. It doesn't know if you're a chairman or a president or an administrator or a manager or a CEO or a founder. The market has no sympathy for your poor background or your rich status. You may be a celeb, a star or a hero somewhere else, but the market couldn't care less. The market couldn't care less whether you're a chief market strategist or a currency analyst or a senior analyst or an official analyst or a coach or a fund manager or a website manager or an accomplished programmer or a software developer or a financial journalist. The market has no regards or honour for who or what you are. The only person the market respects is the person that cuts his losses.

When you see professional traders dashing themselves against the floor of their trading rooms and crying like a baby, it's because they don't cut their losses. When you see a pro trader running to a medical doctor for help; while the doctor says there's nothing wrong with her/him, it's because they doesn't cut their losses.

The best trader in the world is excellent at cutting his losses. When a trade is opened according to a technical or fundamental signal, the best trader opens his trade. However, if there's a loss, he quickly closes the trade. There's no hope or question or argument from the best trader. When a trade doesn't work, he closes it. But another trader – the crazy speculator – argues in favour of significantly losing positions.

Losses are like weeds in a garden while profits are like flowers in the garden. We want to remove our weeds and water our flowers. We don't want to water our weeds and remove our flowers, but according to cold reality, many traders remove their flowers by cutting their profits and water their weeds by allowing their losses to run.

Your ability to cut your losses when they're still insignificant is the most important aspect of your trading career. It's the greatest determinant of your everlasting success, your ability to survive losing streaks (which all proficient traders must inevitably face occasionally) and the possibility of ending up being profitable.

Someone with 80% accuracy will lose their money eventually if they fail to cut their losses while someone with 40% accuracy will end up winning eventually if they do cut losses. When 80% profits are cut and 20% losses are run, they ends up losing money because the 20% losses that aren't controlled can take away all the profits and provide further negativity. When the 60% losses are cut and 40% profits are allowed to run, they ends up making money.

Triumphant traders focus on what they can really control, i.e. their losses (plus profits), knowing full well that their overall success has nothing to do with their strategy which simply shows them when to buy or when to sell. The knowledge of fundamentals, technicals, Elliot Wave, Fibonacci, programming, etc. can't help you if you fail to cut your losses. When an Elliot Wave company makes forecasts and loses, they can be saved only by cutting their losses. Decades of experiences can't help you unless you are good at cutting your losses. Failure to cut your losses will eventually lead to frustration.

Great fundamental figures like Non-farm Payroll have sent some people to their grave because they bet too big and failed to cover their losses. On the other hand, these great fundamental figures have benefitted sane speculators as well.

If you believe in scalping or robots or candlestick patterns, don't forget that the ability to cut your loss while it's small is the ultimate thing. When you enter a trade based on a Hanging Man (Hammer), you might later see it as a Sitting Man (Fata Morgana) if you don't cut your losses. Whether you follow signals or copy trades, cut your losses. Whether you use five-minute charts, or 30-minute charts, or hourly charts, or four-hour charts or daily charts, cut your losses.

You shouldn't bet big in the first place: only bet very small. When the small bet proves to be wrong, then exit with a small loss. This is your life insurance in the market. A small loss that's allowed to run can metamorphose into a gargantuan negativity.

When I place a trade and it loses, I exit at a predetermined level.

When I place another trade and it loses, I exit at a predetermined level.

When I place another trade and it loses, I exit at a predetermined level.

When I place another trade and it loses, I exit at a predetermined level!

When I place another trade and it loses, I exit at a predetermined level!!

When I place another trade and it loses, I exit at a predetermined level!!!

Whenever I see a weed, I don't allow it to grow. I can continue losing, and usually I don't go down more than 5% in the worst-case scenario. After all, the existence of my account is the most important thing, not the profits on it. When a winning streak comes around, I quickly recover. This is the most effective way to make uncertainties my ally.

With a series of stop loss triggers, breakeven triggers, trailing stop triggers and take profit triggers (alternating themselves randomly), I'm sure to move ahead in the long run, no matter how slowly.

You remain victorious as long as you cut your losses without hesitation. Last month, I made a profit of 950 pips as a result of cutting my losses. I'm no better than other traders – neither is my strategy. I realise that cutting my losses is what I must do in order to make profits consistently and enjoy permanent success as a trader. Ability to cut losses is a huge edge indeed! Please don't let your competitor know about this.

The quote below ends this chapter:

"Cut Your Losses Short and Let Your Winners Run,' is the salvation of our trading plans. Since we will both win and lose, big winners outshine small losses every time... Here's a rule we can take to the bank: Whenever you identify HOPE as the primary reason for holding a position, CLOSE IT IMMEDIATLY!" – Bob Robertson

Chapter 44: Greek Debt Crisis and its Effect on Your Investment Accounts

JPY CHF

"When I put on a trade, all I expect is that something will happen." – Mark Douglas

I watched the events in the Eurozone with great interest. I didn't write about the Greek debt crisis at the time because I wanted to see how things turned out. Many economists and financial journalists have written interesting articles about this issue, stating the causes, effects and possible consequences. I don't think repetition is mandatory.

What happened to Greece is what a nation eventually suffers if their government can't spend within its means. The US government is another good example of a government that can't spend within its means, and wise people now ponder the dire/grim consequences that can result in future.

Greece has serious economic problems, and they continue to this day.

Greek Withdrawal from the Eurozone

Experts debated whether Greece would eventually quit or be forced to quit the Eurozone. So far that hasn't happened but anything is possible. Of course, if it did happen with would have grave effects.

It is expected that if Greece withdrew from the Eurozone, the withdrawal would have a great impact on the Greek economy,

Eurozone economy and world economy. But no matter what happened, the sun will continue to rise in the east and set in the west. I didn't expect any serious effects in the currency markets.

Current and Future Effects of Greek Debt Crisis on Forex

Since the media started shouting about the Greek debt crisis, there haven't been any serious effects on the Forex market. The press will always try to find something to write about and whenever the market moves, analysts will try to pinpoint causes for the movement.

The market has a knack for going against people's expectation. Events that people don't anticipate are what cause surprise moves, not events that people anticipate. People didn't anticipate the unprecedented CHF pairs volatility and there were surprise consequences. Another instance of an event that caused surprise movements was the last major earthquake in Japan, which also caused nuclear fallout.

There are years in which the markets move very strongly (like 2008) and there are years in which the markets don't move very strongly (like 2014). Speculators, especially trend-followers, find it easier to harness decent gains when the markets trend strongly.

When the market goes into an equilibrium phase, then sooner or later, there will be an increase in volatility. Conversely, a strong trending movement would eventually lead to low volatility and more predictable outcome. Time indeed factors in economic events and resulting financial consequences.

During May-June 2015, there was low volatility in the market and as a result of that, trend-following strategies suffered. Nevertheless, a measure of volatility returned to the Forex market after the end of June 2015.

Someone who has seen oceans and seas will definitely find a pool in the bathroom negligible. On 29 June 2015, the EUR pair and JYP pairs gapped downwards massively. They later bounced upwards and began to trend downwards the following day. They then consolidated until the end of the week. The same price action was repeated on EUR pair and JPY pairs the following weeks, though the downwards gaps were less significant than the gaps of the previous week.

What happened in the market at that time is nothing special, and nothing special happened in the following weeks and months. Any movements or gaps were no more serious than what we saw earlier in the year.

Many Will Survive the Markets Unpredictability, You Can Too

Some people wanted to stay away from EUR pairs, even though there was no movement on them that was more serious than the movement on AUD pairs, NZD pairs, CAD pairs and JPY pairs. Don't expect any surprises when the public are anticipating them. Surprises come when the public don't anticipate them.

EUR pairs continued to move up and down – as usual – and there was no great deal about that. What happened to EUR pairs on 29 June 2015 had an adverse effect on me. I had three long positions that were all stopped out at 0.75% loss (0.25% X 3 = 0.75%). Was there a big deal in that?

What happened on 6 July had positive effect on my short trades and I gained 2.0%. Again, there was no big deal in that. The market may move slowly against you or in your favour. The market may move fast against you or in your favour, but you'll be fine as long as you truncate your negativity.

The lesson is that you must remain faithful to your positive expectancy trading method – in times of losses and in times of gains. Life isn't a matter of holding good cards but of playing poor cards well. Nowadays, no trader has been dealt perfect market conditions. Often, the secret to gaining control is to both accept those circumstances and manage your trades within the limitations the markets impose on you.

As long as portfolios are concerned, many traders will survive the uncertainties of the future. May you survive as well.

So the Greek debt crisis should not have had any adverse impact on your accounts, if you knew how to control risk. That's the beauty of trading.

Waiter, another bottle of Pepsi, please!

This chapter finishes with the quote below:

"Traders who devote less time to trying to beat the markets and more to mastering their own behaviour and emotion will often outperform those who go in all guns blazing. Trading at the end of the day is a long-term educational process and understanding this and having the patience to develop your skills properly will prove more fruitful in the long run." – Ryhun Rahman

Chapter 45: Leverage Isn't a Bad Thing

AUDGBP

"The point [is] that a trader has to master their psychology to allow him or her to take many small losses, trade through drawdowns, and let winners run beyond expectations." – **Markham Gross**

Some people preach against leverage because of their own faults. They use trading methodologies that ultimately make average losses that are bigger than average profits, while they should be doing the opposite. While we may find it difficult at first (the same was true of me), controlling losses and making trading decisions are very easy when they become our nature.

In order to know what leverage is in trading, plus the advantages in using it, you can search for the information yourself. However, experienced traders should understand what leverage is. Leverage isn't a bad thing – it's irrational use of leverage that's a bad thing.

So I recommend the use of leverage. When leverage is used with strict money management, a heart-warming balance is then found between decent profits and risk control. For example, I use a leverage of 1:100. However, I risk only 0.25% per trade: which means that I use only 0.01 lots for a $2000-account, with a stop of 50 pips per trade. With an account that's less than $2,000, I'll recommend conversion to cents, for greater safety.

The greatest achievement in trading is controlling the treacherous statistics called drawdowns, not making profits, for profits are easy to make but difficult to retain. For example, if you made a profit of 10%

in this month, you could start experiencing losses in the first and/or the second week of the next month (as is true of any trading approach you might adopt). A proof of your proficiency then lies in your ability to lose as little money as possible, going down by, say, 2%-4% maximum. With this, it's easier for you to bounce back when the strategy enters another encouraging winning streak. However, a bad trader would lose between 10%-40% or even more during such a transitory losing streak. What's the benefit of gaining 20% this month and losing 55% next month?

It's a good thing to help our friends and well-wishers to be the best they can be in their trading careers – hence my books and articles. Directly or indirectly, we benefit when our friends and acquaintances become successful. If your friend doesn't become a king, you won't become a friend of a king.

The quote below ends this chapter:

"The problem is adjusting expectations so that your psyche survives long enough for you to be around when the big winner appears. The majority of traders quit simply because expectations and reality are out of alignment." – Chris Tate

Chapter 46: What Every Trader Must Know About Drawdowns

USD NZD

"However, it is pleasant to win over the long term. Contrary to popular opinion, losses are part of winning. Take sports for example." – **Markham Gross**

A drawdown is the peak-to-trough decline during a specific record period of an investment, fund or commodity. A drawdown is usually quoted as the percentage between the peak and the trough. A drawdown is measured from the time a retrenchment begins to when a new high is reached. This method is used because a valley can't be measured until a new high occurs. Once the new high is reached, the percentage change from the old high to the smallest trough is recorded (definition source: Investopedia.com).

As you can see, drawdowns (or roll-downs) are periods when you experience losses and your account goes down. If you open an account with $10, 000 and it drops to $9,200, then you experience a drawdown of 8%.

Causes of Drawdowns

Let's put the issue of trading with no stops and high risk aside. Let's imagine someone is using a good strategy that makes him cut his loss at 50 pips and run a profit until it reaches 200 pips. That's a good trading idea which makes money when currency pairs trend nicely. Nevertheless, when a period of drawdowns comes, more stops are triggered and take profit levels are hardly reached. The few take profit levels that are reached are too few to recover the too many stops that are triggered. You open many trades and they move in your favour by a few or several pips and then turn negative, hitting your stop. For days, weeks, or months, false breakouts are not a curiosity and sustained trending movement are scarce.

Trading ideas that let profits run are the best, but they generally suffer when the markets enter equilibrium phases.

As in real life, doing the right things doesn't always make you appear smart. In fact, you may sometimes look stupid by doing the right things. A trader that uses a stop may appear stupid when they are stopped out on a trade that eventually reverses and turns positive. A trader may appear stupid when a position they are trying to ride fails to meet its target, turning from positivity to negativity. But in the end, we will reap the benefits of doing the rights things.

Soon, a time comes when the situation changes and the person will recover the losses within days, weeks or months.

Treacherous Statistics

Look at the long-term results of the strategies below:

Strategy A:
Growth: 343.80%
Drawdown: 37.45%
Monthly: 19.09%

Strategy B:
Growth: 119.40
Drawdown: 22.08%
Monthly: 10.51%

Strategy C:
Growth: 12.04%
Drawdown: 11.16%
Monthly: 0.49%

You can see that the strategies above have made nice profits in the long run, but not without roll-downs. Strategy A has earned a profit of 343.80% over the years, but it also went through periods of losses amounting to 37.45%. The users of the strategies obviously deal with the roll-downs successfully; otherwise they'd have disappeared.

One marketer was recently creating hype that he had a strategy that could turn $500 into a growing monthly income. As you know, the job of marketers is to emphasize the bright side of what they sell, while glossing over the dark side. It's like when a religious preacher is telling people nice things that will happen to them if they join their religion, without telling them the reality that religious people are not immune from suffering – when an earthquake occurs, it doesn't avoid the religious people in the region.

I never tried that hyped strategy – though I've tested over 250 strategies in my entire career. There's no perfect strategy and there won't be one. All excellent trading strategies experience drawdowns. All super traders experience drawdowns, albeit victoriously in the end.

Sadly, the subject of drawdowns is the least mentioned in the trading industry, and there's only scanty literature about the subject, in spite of the fact that it's one of the most important topics in trading. Drawdowns must be experienced from time to time by all traders irrespective of age, intelligence, expertise, years of experience, risk control ability and strategies. This is where the majority of traders fail. Your ability to deal with drawdowns successfully is the greatest determinant of the end game and is your ability to enjoy a long-lasting career.

The smaller a loss is, the easier it is to recover. The bigger a loss is, the more difficult it is to recover.

There are periods when you'll make money; there are periods when you'll lose money and there are periods when your performance will be flat (you won't go up or down). There's no way around this fact. There is no way around the fact that you must sustain losses that you will then eventually recover. Flat and drawdown periods may even be longer than you expect. Switching strategies isn't the way out. Can a rolling stone gather any moss?

That's why it's unrealistic to set a weekly or monthly target in a world in which you can't really predict the future. That's why it's realistic to open a trade only after you have imagined the worst-case scenario. With that kind of mindset, you'll realise the folly of not using stops and the folly of trading with large lot sizes. However, most of us have serious psychological and emotional problems.

One of the most frustrating things is to keep on trading when you keep on making losses. Your hope of a monthly income will be dashed and your courage will evaporate. The frustration can even become more intense, especially if you live in a country where you have to generate your own electricity and fuel is extremely scarce and expensive.

What Good Traders Experience

I remember what happened to me in 2011. I was making good profits for about four months: up to 30% (6,000 pips). Then suddenly, the market conditions changed and I was having loss after loss. I kept on managing my risk, being faithful to the system I used. The losing periods lasted for about three months and I went down from 30% pips to 15%, and suddenly... the market conditions became favourable again and I finished that year with 49% profits.

In a typical year, you can make 10% in January and 6% in February. You can make 3% in March and lose 9% in April. You can lose 4.5% in May and lose an additional 5% in June. You can gain 4% in July and lose 4% in August. You can gain 11% in September and gain another 6.5% in October. You can gain 15% in November and finish December with another 2.5%. How much would the trader end up with in the year? This is the reality of trading, which you must accept or go do something else.

Many so called Forex traders are gamblers who think they're good. They lose hugely or earn margin calls during drawdowns.

Anton Kreil says you will have about three months (or more or less) in a year in which you'll experience drawdowns no matter what you do. How do you explain this to your investors? How do you explain this to your family?

When you limit a loss, you accept the fact that it won't have any major impact on your portfolio anytime, no matter how terrible the situation may be. You can check your account history or past trading results in order to reassure yourself, knowing full well that your system will soon start working again because it worked in the past. You'll be encouraged to keep on taking new signals (for you don't know the ones that would win and recover your losses), maintaining discipline and calm.

To be a permanently victorious trader, you must control your losses and limit your roll-downs. It may be emotionally satisfying to refuse to accept a mistake and ignore the use of stops, and the temptation to do silly things will balloon. In most cases, prices may go back to your entry points after harrowing periods of waiting and hope, which may be longer than normal. There will also be cases in which the hopes are dashed as prices refuse to come back in your favour, going further and further against you instead. All the profits plus the capital you have can vanish. All market veterans acknowledge that the importance of loss control can't be emphasized enough, because that's the reason why over 95% of traders can't be successful as traders.

On Trade2win.com, Barjon says, "Perhaps all this makes it sound as though our trader's reasoning will be spot on or that he is a fortune teller who can foresee the future. There is no such trader. All trading is about making assumptions based on experience of what has happened in similar circumstances in the past. Those assumptions may be right or they may be wrong and from the business perspective the aim is to gain the necessary advantage when they are right and limit the damage when they are not."

This chapter is ended by the quotes below:

"Our worst case scenario for the basic strategy is where the trader can lose 70 per cent of the time with a reward-risk ratio of 3:1. With these statistics the trader can still be consistently profitable. The winners take care of the losers." – Manesh Patel

"The difference between top-notch winning traders and those who barely get by is the attitude they take toward losses. Trading is a tough business where setbacks and losses are commonplace. If you aren't careful, you can feel beaten, knocked down, and afraid to get back up. It may be difficult at times, but it is often necessary to forget about the past." – Joe Ross

Chapter 47: HYIPs – Solutions for Traders?

CADEUR

"Illusions are something pleasant. The disadvantage is that they tend to burst like a bubble." – Wolfgang Kurz

"It is true that the market is brutal to most of the people who challenge it. But so is Mount Everest, and that should not – and does not – stop people from trying to reach the top. What is expected of a mountain or a market is only that it has no favourites – that it treats all challengers as equals." – Mark Minervini

Investopedia describes a high-yield investment program (HYIP) as a fraudulent investment scheme that purports to deliver extraordinarily high returns on investment. High-yield investment schemes often advertise yields of more than 100% per year in order to lure in victims. In reality, these high-yield investment programs are Ponzi schemes and the organizers aim to steal the money invested.

Wonder Banks

Another name for a HYIP is "a wonder bank.' Isn't it a wonder that one will double one's money in a month or a quarter or a year without lifting a finger, as compared to the very low returns promised by legitimate banks? In my country, some wonder banks existed during 2006-2008. They promised high returns every month, quarter or six months. Some investors gave money to them and while certain people got their money back, most people were unable to get their money back. The wonder banks failed and such entities were subsequently banned. It's one of the reasons why most people hate online trading.

That's why one sage says that extraordinary claims require extraordinary proof, because if something sounds too good to be true, it probably is.

There are 'wonder banks' all over the world and most of them are scammers running Ponzi schemes. Recently, one wonder bank got access to the subscribers' base of a legitimate financial organization. The wonder bank promised returns of 500% within five hours if an individual advert recipient deposited any amount between $1,000 and $1,000,000 with them. Did you need to be advised before you knew the wonder bank was set up by scammers? If their claims were genuine, then there would be no more poor people on earth. If their claims were genuine, they wouldn't need to solicit the members of the public for this kind of investment program.

Shady persons promised such returns because it fit the mindset of most people. 1% returns per month doesn't fit the mindset of most people and thus, they find it difficult to accept. On the other hand, sane people will agree that 1% returns per month are good and one can be rich with that ultimately.

10% per month without a single losing month is impossible. 1.27% profit per day is impossible. No company would promise that and still be in business for a long time. I'm not saying that 10% per month or 1.27% is impossible in the short-term (though that's based on pure luck and successful trading needs far more than luck), but I'm saying that there's no firm that can last long aiming for that.

How long will it take a unit of real estate to appreciate by 100%? What about fixed deposits and bonds? Could you force 5% appreciation on each of them on monthly basis? Yet, most traders can't even accept 5% profits per month.

One respected friend once asked me how much I make per month. I mentioned that I target only 1% per month, no matter my account size, and in some cases I make more than that in several months per year. He was disappointed, for he was expecting me to mention that I make 20%-50% per month. Please see the quote above: Illusions are something really pleasant.

Another wise fund manager recently told me that it's difficult to manage money for greedy people. Some of his investors complained that he didn't make enough profits: not that he didn't make profits, but that he didn't make enough profits. They weren't even thankful for the existence of their capital. It's clear that these investors would be risking too high if they were to trade themselves and they would end up blowing the accounts. People don't appreciate the existence of what they have until they lose it.

Someone nicknamed Handle123 on Elitetrader.com says that the trader "is like the tortoise and the rabbit, no wonder the tortoise lives to be over hundred years old, he learned to go slow and don't take dumb chances of moving a foot before knowing if it can be life threatening risk. And rabbits have little defence other than speed, but many more rabbits in the stew pot than tortoises."

Please think about the preceding paragraph. Do you want to be like a tortoise or like a rabbit?

Anyone who believes in excessively high returns over short periods of time isn't psychologically prepared to make money. They can't even settle for 2% growth per month. They would rather go for at least 100% per month (unrealistic expectations). In fact, such a person would end up being a loser in life.

I end this chapter with the quote below:

"The best investment you can make is in your own education. Unless you are educated in how the markets work, how to invest in or trade shares, the psychology behind trading and investing, and which derivatives can give you the best returns, you have little hope of being profitable as a trader." – Louise Bedford

Chapter 48: Online Trading Is No Sin

EUR NZD

"I've not failed. I've just found 10,000 ways that won't work." – Thomas Edison

"...If trading is only about money, you have very little chance of success." – Dr Van K Tharp

In recent times, some people have questioned the morality of online trading. Obviously, the question comes from lack of real understanding of trading.

Trading had long been done before the advent of the internet: the internet technology simply made it easier and more easily accessible. In other areas of life and business, most things that were done before the advent of the internet have now gone online. Think about hotel reservations and university applications as examples.

There are different types of markets and Forex is just one of them. For example, one can speculate on the prices of agricultural products online and the risky nature of doing that doesn't make it immoral.

It's clear that trading online isn't a sin – just as reading religious literature online and joining a service online isn't a sin. We can now listen to sermons online, which wasn't possible 50 year ago. Does that make it a sin?

With fast advances in science and technology, the ways we do business will forever keep on changing and evolving. Several decades ago, trading was done mainly in the pit, but things have changed now. Thanks to the internet.

James Altucher says that when he was 13 years old, the job he's doing now didn't exist. His daughter might end up doing a job that didn't exist when she also was 13 years old. Those who don't adapt to the changing technological ways of life will pay a heavy price for their myopic views.

At the beginning of his book, *Tough Times Never Last but Tough People Do,* Robert H. Schuller (RIP) mentions what happened to his dad as a farmer. All his labour, crops, property and so on, were all destroyed by a violent storm. All his hard labour was in vain. Does that make it immoral to be a farmer?

Apart from the fact that there are certain factors beyond the control of the farmer (like weather conditions, poor harvest and economic forces); the farmer can sell at loss or at profit. That doesn't make it a sin to be a farmer. In fact, farming is a noble profession. Trading is a noble profession too.

Robert's dad continued working as a farmer. Though he seemed totally hopeless and helpless, there was inner hope in him. What happened to him later? He was already a successful trader when he died.

One popular celebrity said she doesn't believe in marriage. She was married about 32 years ago and the marriage crashed in less than two years. Since then, she's been preaching against marriage. Certain male and female celebrities also don't believe in marriage. Does that make it wrong to get married? I know many people whose marriages are super successful. Marriage isn't compulsory; neither is it evil.

A trading legend makes money trading stock and loses money trading futures, options and Forex, and he concludes that one can't make money from Forex. Another legend that makes money from stocks, options and Forex says they're excellent markets. What can you conclude from that? It means that the fact that one person is losing in a market doesn't mean that others can't make money from the same market.

The world-famous Dr Van K Tharp has been using what he calls "oneness formula" to transform lives of traders. He mentions something like an inner guide who leads and guides traders to become successful not only in trading, but in other areas of life. According to him, if you are not organized or tend to procrastinate or run away and hide each time you encounter some major psychological issue that impacts your life, then you don't have a chance at becoming a successful trader.

This is what one of the beneficiaries of Van Tharp's works has to say: *"There was a time I identified a negative association about God and trading, and sometimes I felt uncomfortable with the idea of trading. But then, I learned how it was just a belief. Just that. And I can always change any belief I want, and when I see things in a different way, there is no conflict between God and trading."* – J. Ernesto D. M. (Source: Vantharp.com).

Anne-Marie Baiynd is a successful trader as well as religious. This is what she has to say: *"I strive for God to be in charge of my life. I live as a speck of dust, flawed, sinful and self-serving by nature. My existence is defined by emptiness without the existence of the All Mighty God. I am accepted and loved, nonetheless, and that creates within me, a great joy and contentment knowing that all my triumphs and successes come from God."*

Sir John Templeton, a market wizard, also said: *"We are trying to persuade people that no human has yet grasped 1% of what can be known about spiritual realities. So we are encouraging people to start using the same methods of science that have been so productive in other areas, in order to discover spiritual realities."* (Interview with Financial Intelligence Report).

Bruce Bower, a hedge fund manager, is a Christian who goes to Church regularly. Joes Ross, one of the most experienced and the most eclectic traders in the word, is a good Christian. There are good Muslims who are also traders. There are good Hindus, Buddhists, etc. who are good traders as well. There are proficient traders all over the world who belong to major or minor religions. This is a level playing field.

Failure is a Good Thing

Please see the quotes from Thomas Edison and from Dr Van K Tharp above. Failure is embedded in success. It's part of success. It gives you opportunity to do your trading intelligently. Failure helps you to see how not to trade. When you do trading and fail, you learn how not to trade and you use another method. Even if the new method fails, you try another method… Until you come across a trading approach that works for you.

Those hugely successful people that you now envy took risks. They could have failed just like many others, but they were fortunate. If they failed, they would try again and again. Mark Zuckerberg, who thinks of himself as an atheist, says the biggest risk is not taking any risk… In a world that's changing really quickly, the only strategy that is guaranteed to fail is not taking risks.

The fact that you fail or the majority fails in something doesn't make it sinful. Good trading is a serious business, not a gamble. However, it's not without risk, just like any other things in life.

Trading is definitely no sin. Good trading principles aren't against any other religions.

This chapter ends with the quotes below:

"I pray to Jesus Christ every day, but that is not a means to handle trading. I ask Him to guide my decisions, and that I would do my investing to glorify Him. Because I use my rules, there is little, if any, stress over trading. My processes are designed to take my emotion out of my infrequent buying and selling." – David J. Merkel

"I love the markets: They are alive, they move, they have spiritual energy. They are an expression of the universe and of course they are my mirror, just as they are your mirror. They are the medium through which I choose to express myself and

grow. I am grateful for this and the technology that allows me to participate and trust that the markets will always be there, no matter what change is upon us in the coming years." – Mercedes Oestermann van Essen (Source: Thebuddhisttrader.com)

Chapter 49: Handling Equilibrium (Trendless) Markets and Losing Streaks

CHF AUD

"You can't congratulate yourself on your wins. Just like you can't despair over your losses. Success is not one event. Too many one-hit wonders realised this too late." – James Altucher

This chapter was written with traders who control their risk and follow sound trading plans in mind. Controlling one's risk and following sound trading plans don't make us immune to losing periods; they simply ensure that we come out of the losing periods successfully.

An equilibrium market is also called a consolidating or a sideways market. This is a condition in which the movement in the market is almost flat and it is difficult to make money from such a market. When a market moves strongly, position trading, swing trading and intraday trading methodologies make easy money as traders cut their losses and run their profits.

But there are times when the market doesn't move strongly, experiencing a pause in the movement. Even in markets that trend strongly like Forex markets, equilibrium phases would be observed from time to time. This is the time in which most targets wouldn't be reached and stops would often be triggered, because the movement of the price would be short-term and erratic in most cases.

For those who follow the trend or look for strong movements, equilibrium phases (which are inevitable) are when losing streaks occur. During this phase, trading strategies go out of sync with the markets and trades tend to go into negative territories without going positive, as those that first turn positive eventually go negative without hitting the targets. During this phase, stops – whether tight or wide – are frequently hit and targets are rarely reached.

In trendless markets, most fundamental figures would simply be shrugged off by the markets.

But one thing should be remembered: a period of low volatility will be replaced by a period of high volatility and the other way round. Strategies that go out of sync with the market will eventually move in sync with it and vice versa. There is no strategy that always works in all market conditions: a strategy that works well in equilibrium markets may fail during strong trending movements.

The trick is to know what to do when there is an equilibrium phase and trading results are poor. We want to lose as little as possible out of our accumulated profits and we want to recover as quickly as rationally possible when things turn in our favour. The less our drawdowns in equilibrium markets, the faster our recovery will be when things turn in our favour. We don't know when an equilibrium phase will start and when it will end. We just perceive it when it happens and the duration may be shorter or longer than we think.

When Not To Let Profits Run

Let me give you an example of how I deal with losing streaks and equilibrium markets.

Since I target at least 200 pips per trade, I discover a period of equilibrium markets when only one or two or even none of my targets are hit in a week and the same results are repeated in the following week. In this period, I undergo negligible drawdowns instead of gains. This is when I'll start cutting my profit per trade after the trade is about eight to ten hours old. With this, further drawdowns will be limited and some profits are prevented from going into negative territory. This is my only trading rule that changes temporarily for the rest of the month. I do this for only two weeks and then go back to running my profits as long as possible.

The same rule applies in a new month: I let my profits run throughout the month unless the first two weeks are negative. When the markets move strongly, about three or four or more of my targets would be reached every week; plus targets are sometimes reached within hours or a few days after opening of trades.

Some expert traders simply stop trading for two weeks or the month when they lose a predetermined amount of money, like 5%-6% of their accounts. The reason why I stay in the market is that I don't know when there will be strong breakouts/significant volatility in the markets. Since I try to trade around the territories where prices may go out of balance, I sometimes catch strong movements.

A Future Without Worries

When we undergo troubling circumstances, we can easily become discouraged. At such times, we can be comforted and strengthened by reflecting on the blessings we've enjoyed so far as traders. Often, negative feelings are not the results of our circumstances but how we view them.

Unless you have expectations that are too high, too soon, you don't need to get disappointed during equilibrium phases. A roaring lion kills no game.

As in real life, doing the right things doesn't always make you appear smart. In fact, you may sometimes look stupid by doing the right things. A trader that uses a stop may appear stupid when they're stopped out on a trade that eventually reverses and turns positive. A trader may appear stupid when a position they're trying to ride fails to meet its target, turning from positivity to negativity. But in the end, you'll reap the benefits of doing the rights things. In your trading career, the best is yet to come.

As someone once said, the return of your money is more important than the return on your money. The rain is more important than the dew.

This chapter ends with the quote below:

"Many traders, especially beginning traders, seem to think that they have to trade all the time if they want to make money. Very often the opposite is true. A good trader is a patient trader, because he knows that 'the long run' is longer than we think." – Andy Jordan

Chapter 50: The Beauty of Trading

NZD GBP

"You do not need a PhD in math or physics to be successful in the stock market, just the right knowledge, a good work ethic, and discipline." – Mark Minervini

Imagine. There's someone who borrowed a total of $13 million to make a movie. She is a credit officer at a big financial institution who has helped many candidates secure loans to finance their ambitions. She herself was unable to get a loan to finance the production of her movie. In fact, it took her more than six years to get money to produce her movie. After going to the States to learn how to direct movies, she had to sell all her property and borrow money from some friends and banks, before they could get the needed $13 million to finance the movie. The movie could have been a crashing failure, but fortunately, it was a roaring success. This courageous woman took a great risk.

Can you see the length people can go in order to achieve their dreams? The risk I take as a trader is even far less than this, with the assurance that my possibility of success is high because I'm a veteran trader.

Have you been touched by sadness in trading? You might feel that's a problem without solution. But there is a solution – namely, the necessary mindset and principles that are necessary for your happiness. A losing period is a terrible problem, but there are wonderful solutions to that.

If people discourage you, you could begin to think that the sacrifices you make in your trading career aren't worthwhile or that you can't attain permanent success. Since we're surrounded by people that don't understand the truth about trading, we must strive to keep our focus on the ultimate goals.

If You Can Draw a Straight Line, You Can Become a Successful Trader

This subheading was taken from one of the titles written by DbPhoenix of Trade2win.com. Contrary to what most people tend to think, you can become a permanently successful trader if you have a positive expectancy methodology and a winning attitude.

The road to profitability is to think positively and take steps. This doesn't mean that your steps would often lead to what you want. There are times when you'll feel that you can't become a winning speculator. You can even contemplate quitting. I know this. It's happened to me. There were times when I was discouraged by poor trading results and I thought of abandoning my trading career.

Nonetheless, I was aware of the potency of perseverance and so I didn't quit. After many years of grappling with the markets, I'm eventually able to make money in the markets, surviving trendless and choppy periods and moving smoothly ahead when the markets trend strongly. I'm now able to keep my funds safe despite the vagaries of the markets. Sometimes, I make more than I even anticipate in a month.

Forex to removed me from poverty and launched me onto my way to financial freedom.

Conclusion

Like the veterans of the markets, we don't feel that the years we spend trying to bring our best trading self are a waste of time. Rather, we're sure that the challenges are transitory and the rewards are permanent. I think of someone like Adam Jowett, who is an entrepreneur and a developer who trades anywhere possible, like in the toilet, in the bus and in his garage. I know another trader who travels worldwide and trades on the go, raking in lots of money in the process.

This chapter ends by the quote below:

"Learning by trading may be the school of hard knocks, but in the end that is the best school you can attend. Just keep standing up over and over again, until you learn how to profit. Until that point, trade small and make sure to stay in the game. Make sure you will still be there once the profits arrive. And do not forget to enjoy the ride." – Marko Graenitz

Conclusion

AUDEUR

You Don't Need to Stop Trading

There are many people who used to be traders. They started trading because they thought it was easy and because they thought they'd strike it rich. Nevertheless, they discovered that trading isn't easy and after they dashed their heads into the rock many times, they gave up.

Whenever they come across successful traders, they wonder how those traders manage to keep consistent.

Their notion is simple. If they can't do trading successfully, they feel no one else can do it, or very few people can do it. They gave up and they expected others to give up. Surprisingly, some speculators don't give up. In fact, they have methodologies that help them make money in the market and they like that. Most of the methodologies are their secrets.

The World of Trading is Full of Hypocrisy

How long would people talk about their profits alone and hide their losses? When NZD pairs moved maniacally on 19 October 2017, I saw how many people posted the profits they made. But none of them would ever post losses they made. Very few traders would post their losses. The world of trading is full of hypocrisy.

When someone makes 300 USD or let's say, 300 pips, they post it on forums, WhatsApp groups, Facebook, etc. When the person makes a loss, they remain silent about it. That's why some rookies think trading is easy – just because everyone is talking about profits.

FACT: Trading isn't easy, though the marketer would want you to believe otherwise. Success is, nonetheless possible.

Liberate Yourself with Trading Realities

You will never find a perfect trading system or signals service. You can't avoid losses. But you'll be OK as long as your average losses are smaller than your average profits.

I recently showed one of my trainees my trading results. I placed a trade, I lost it (-1%).

I placed another trade, I lost it (-1%).

I placed another trade and I lost it (-1%).

I placed another trader and I lost it (-1%).

Four losses in a row (-4%).

I placed the fifth trade and I won it (+6.9%). I let my profit run.

You see, I made sure that I limited my losses and I let my profits run.

I didn't throw away my strategy because of a transient losing streak, since I know it's a statistical edge.

There are many bogus high probability strategies (manual, automated or semi-automated) that can win 99% of trades in a row. But one big loss would wipe away everything.

Think about the rest. It's up to you.

About the Author

Azeez Mustapha is a trading professional, fund manager, an InstaForex official analyst, a blogger at ADVFN.com, and a freelance author for trading magazines. He works as a trading signals provider at various websites and his numerous articles are posted on many websites such as:www.ituglobalforex.blogspot.com.

Contact: azeez.mustapha@analytics.instaforex.com.

Azeez has published four previous books with ADVFN Books: *Learn From the Generals of the Markets*, *What Super Traders Don't Want You to Know*, *Super Trading Strategies* and *Insights Into the Mindset of Super Traders*. Turn over for more details of these titles.

Also by Azeez Mustapha

Insights into the Mindset of Super Traders

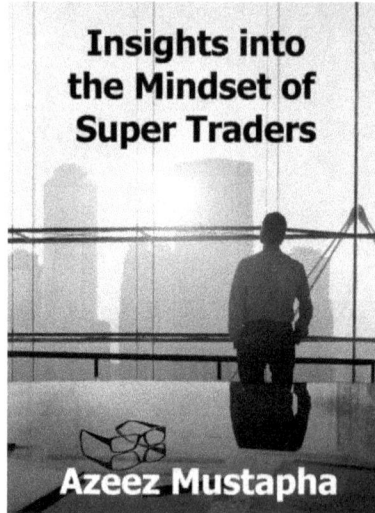

Insights into the Mindset of Super Traders

Azeez Mustapha

Anyone can learn to be a trader – but making a success of it involves more than just pushing Bid and Ask buttons. You need good strategies that will allow you to deal with the vagaries of the market.

It's no secret that the majority of traders lose. But some succeed and become rich, even super-rich. These are the super traders.

Insights into the Mindset of Super Traders reveals the life stories of 20 selected master traders: how they think, how they view the markets and how they make their fortunes. In this follow up to his previous books *Learn From the Generals of the Markets* and *What Super Traders Don't Want You to Know*, Azeez Mustapha gives an overview of their careers and explains what lessons can be drawn from their success.

Learn the insights, approaches and thoughts of the super traders, apply their methods and techniques to your own trading and gain the expertise you need to improve your prospects.

This essential guide could start you on the path to becoming a super trader.

Available in paperback and for the Kindle.

Super Trading Strategies

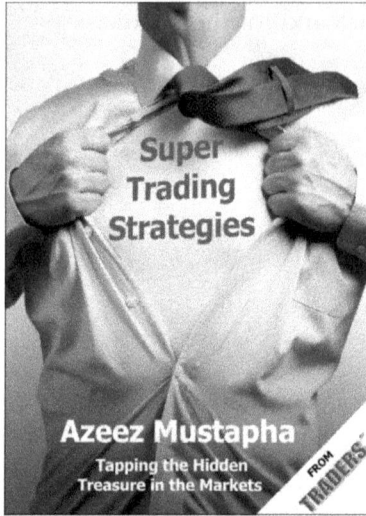

If you want to be a success trading on the Forex markets, you need to know what you are doing. Learning by trial and error can be expensive and one wrong move could wipe you out. You need help to know what strategies work and how they should be used.

Super Trading Strategies gives you a set of concrete and easy-to-use trading strategies that will help you on your way to making money. They all work on the Forex markets, and some are also applicable to the stock and futures markets.

These super trading strategies include short-term, long-term, swing and positions trading strategies. Some are ideal for part-time traders and some for full-time traders.

Each strategy is explained in detail with examples of how they can be used and charts illustrating the currency movements to which they apply. At the end of each chapter, a strategy snapshot summarises what you have learned.

Written by an experienced Forex trader who is also a journalist and writer, *Super Trading Strategies* will help you win the battles of the Forex markets.

The strategies were previously published in TRADERS' magazine.

Available in paperback and for the Kindle.

What Super Traders Don't Want You to Know

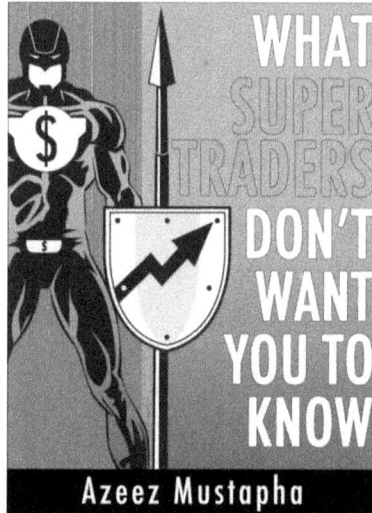

If you want to succeed as a trader, you need to learn the necessary skills.

Risk your money on the markets without knowing what you are doing, and you could lose it all. Just like any other profession, to be a trader requires you to learn from the experts.

What Super Traders Don't Want You To Know profiles twenty-two renowned super traders from around the world, great traders who know what it takes to be successful in the markets. In this follow up to his previous book *Learn From the Generals of the Markets*, Azeez Mustapha gives an overview of their careers and explains what lessons can be drawn from their success.

You can apply their methods and techniques to your own trading, and gain the expertise you need to improve your prospects.

This essential guide could start you on the path to becoming a super trader.

Available in paperback and for the Kindle.

Learn From the Generals of the Market

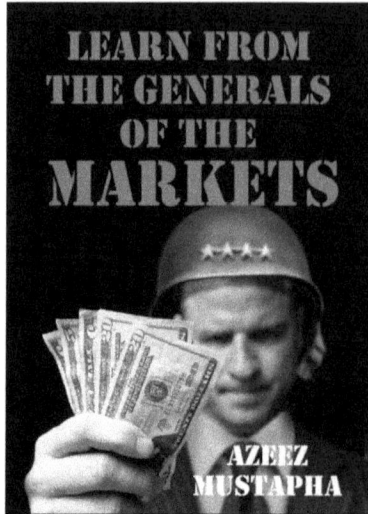

If you want to win on the trading battlefield, you need the right ammunition.

Trading is like any other profession: to succeed, you need to arm yourself with the necessary skills. Enter the arena without knowing what you are doing, and you are sure to lose your money.

You need help from the experts.

Learn From the Generals of the Markets profiles twenty renowned super traders from around the world, great traders who know what it takes to be successful in the markets. The book gives an overview of their careers and explains what lessons can be drawn from their success, so you can apply their methods and techniques to your own trading. It will help you gain the expertise you need to improve your prospects.

This essential guide should be part of every trader's armament.

Available in paperback and for the Kindle.

More Books from ADVFN

Trading Cryptocurrencies: A Beginner's Guide

Bitcoin, Ethereum, Litecoin

by Clem Chambers

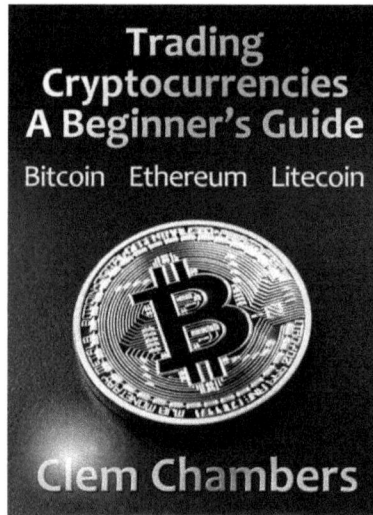

Bitcoin is going wild, with a valuation that has gone from zero to higher than $6,000 in just four years. Altcoins are springing up like mushrooms; some will thrive and others will fade away. Blockchain is the new buzzword that everyone is excited about.

It's the dotcom bubble all over again and if you can trade it and not blow your account up you can make a killing.

But cryptocurrencies are not the same as equities or bonds. They are their own ecosystem and they obey new rules that no-one fully understands. This means there is big risk in trading them – but also the chance of a big reward.

This book tells you everything you need to know about cryptocurrencies – what they are, how they work and how you can make money from them. The author explains how Bitcoin exchanges and trading sites work and walks you through your first purchase of Bitcoins. He talks about trading different cryptocurrencies, market making and the fundamentals of selecting a good coin to buy. He also covers mining cryptocoins, and for those that are interested in the technical aspect of cryptocurrencies and the blockchain he delves into the details behind them.

If you are interested in joining this exciting new area of investing and trading, this book will be an invaluable guide.

Available in paperback and for the Kindle.

The Complete Guide To Successful Financial Markets Trading

Simon Watkins

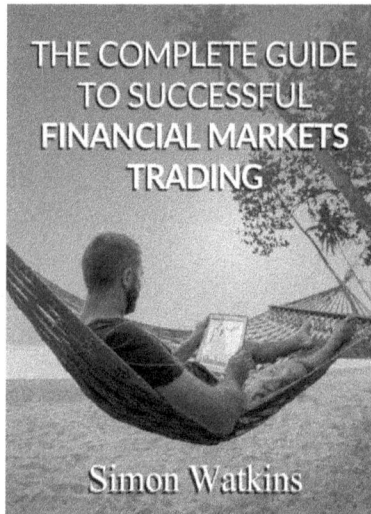

Many people still regard trading the financial markets as a complicated and risky business, but neither of these assumptions are correct. If you know what you are doing and stick to the very basic rules of dealing then there is no reason at all why you cannot make life-changing amounts of money for as long as you keep trading.

The Complete Guide To Successful Financial Markets Trading goes step-by-step through all aspects of trading all major asset classes so that, by the end of it, readers will be in a position to profitably trade whichever of them they wish and, in the process, significantly augment their day-to-day incomes or indeed become full-time financial markets' traders.

Fully illustrated with detailed charts, the book covers the basics of foreign exchange trading, the equities markets, trading in oil and other commodities, technical analysis, and risk/reward management.

Whether you are an experienced trader or just starting out, the information in this book offers you strategies to become one of the winners in the financial markets.

Available in paperback and for the Kindle.

Trade Financial Markets Like The Pros

by Simon Watkins

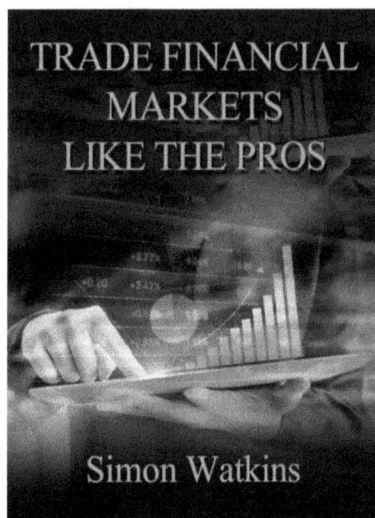

There has never been a more difficult time to make money from trading the markets than now. All of the long-standing foundation stones of the global financial system are in a state of flux: engines of growth, monetary policies and the correlation dynamics between asset classes.

Additionally, each of the four core regional growth engines around the world – the US, the Eurozone, China and Japan – face their own sets of problems, undermining the historic relationships between stocks, bonds and currencies even further.

Given this backdrop, it is more important than ever that traders manage and exploit the few remaining factors in global markets that hold good. This is what this book is about: knowing what these are, exploiting them and banking the profits in a risk/reward efficient manner.

Fully illustrated with detailed charts, *Trade Financial Markets Like The Pros* covers how to balance risk against reward, how to search out correlations between asset classes that offer trading opportunities, and the major factors that could continue to twist financial markets into wildly contradictory modes. It also gives a refresher course in technical analysis and the full range of hedging techniques, including options, to offset possible losses.

Whether you are an experienced trader or just starting out, the information in this book offers you strategies to become one of the winners in the financial markets, and to avoid risking catastrophic losses.

Available in paperback and for the Kindle.

The Great Oil Price Fixes And How To Trade Them

by Simon Watkins

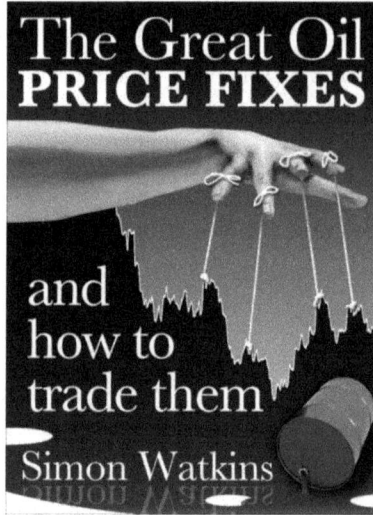

The oil market has been manipulated to an extremely high degree for decades, both overtly and covertly, and given its enduring geopolitical importance that is likely to continue.

Traders need to understand the essential dynamics that drive the global oil market, offering as it does unparalleled opportunities to make returns over and above those of other markets. The oil market is also an essential part of trading FX, equities, bonds and other commodities.

Simon Watkins' book *The Great Oil Price Fixes And How To Trade Them* offers you the knowledge you need. It covers the history of the market, gives you an understanding of the players in the oil game, and provides a solid grounding in the market-specific trading nuances required in this particular field.

The essential elements of the general trading methodology, strategies and tactics that underpin top professional traders are covered with reference to how they can be used to trade in the oil market.

Available in paperback and for the Kindle.

18 Smart Ways to Improve Your Trading

by Maria Psarra

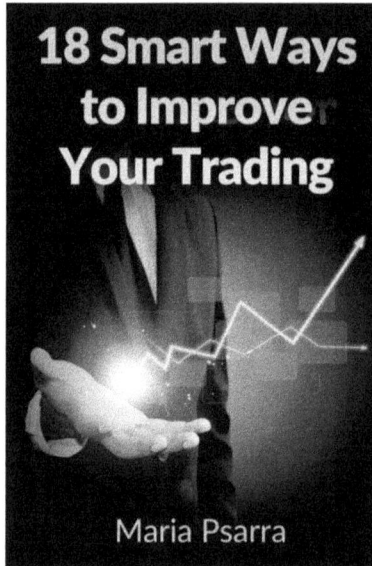

Any trader or investor that says they have never lost money in the markets is too young, too stupid, too inexperienced, or just plain lying to you. Everyone makes mistakes, particularly when starting out as a trader. It's part of the learning curve.

What matters is that you learn from your mistakes. Even better, learn from the mistakes others have made to avoid making them yourself.

18 Smart Ways to Improve Your Trading explains some of the common mistakes traders make and the routines that winning traders use to avoid those errors. The author draws on her many years' experience of trading, both on institutional proprietary trading desks and for herself, and the knowledge she has gained advising professional clients.

In this book she shares her expertise with you. The *18 Smart Ways* include the habits that separate winning traders from losing ones, the secrets to profitable trading and how to deal with the emotional hiccups that cause you to lose in the markets.

If you absorb these lessons then they should make you a better investor or trader.

Originally published as articles in Master Investor magazine.

Available in paperback and for the Kindle.

101 Charts for
Trading Success

by Zak Mir

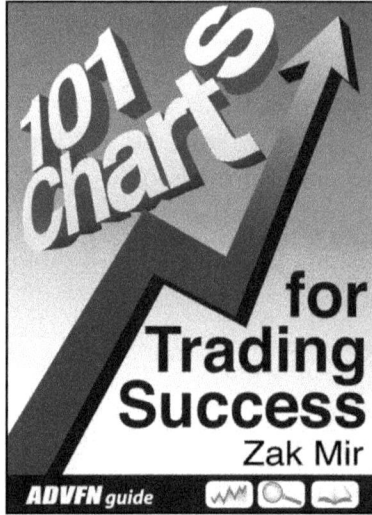

Using insider knowledge to reveal the tricks of the trade, Zak Mir's *101 Charts for Trading Success* explains the most complex set ups in the stock market.

Providing a clear way of predicting price action, charting is a way of making money by delivering high probability percentage trades, whilst removing the need to trawl through company accounts and financial ratios.

Illustrated with easy to understand charts this is the accessible, essential guide on how to read, understand and use charts, to buy and sell stocks. *101 Charts* is a must for all future investment millionaires.

Available in paperback and for the Kindle.

The Game in Wall Street

by Hoyle and Clem Chambers

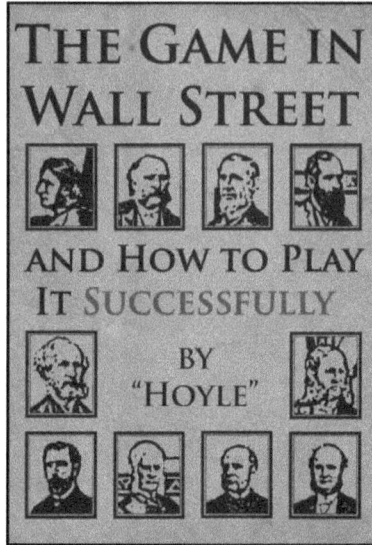

As the new century dawned, Wall Street was a game and the stock market was fixed. Ordinary investors were fleeced by big institutions that manipulated the markets to their own advantage and they had no comeback.

The Game in Wall Street shows the ways that the titans of rampant capitalism operated to make money from any source they could control. Their accumulated funds gave the titans enormous power over the market and allowed them to ensure they won the game.

Traders joining the game without knowing the rules are on a road to ruin. It's like gambling without knowing the rules and with no idea of the odds.

The Game in Wall Street sets out in detail exactly how this market manipulation works and shows how to ride the price movements and make a profit.

And guess what? The rules of the game haven't changed since the book was first published in 1898. You can apply the same strategies in your own investing and avoid losing your shirt by gambling against the professionals.

Illustrated with the very first stock charts ever published, the book contains a new preface and a conclusion by stock market guru Clem Chambers which put the text in the context of how Wall Street operates today.

Available in paperback and for the Kindle.

For more information, go to the ADVFN Books website at www.advfnbooks.com.

ADVFN BOOKS

www.ingramcontent.com/pod-product-compliance
Lightning Source LLC
Chambersburg PA
CBHW060014210326
41520CB00009B/887